UNITED *in* MARRIAGE *by* ONE LORD

UNITED *in* MARRIAGE *by* ONE LORD

God's Wisdom on Intermarriage
in a Multifaith World

GRAHAM ROBERTS

Authentic

United in Marriage by One Lord
By Graham Roberts

First edition 2006
ISBN 81-7362-722-3

Published by
OM Authentic Books, P. O. Box 2190
Secunderabad 500 003,
Andhra Pradesh, India.

Authentic Books, 9 Holdom Avenue
Bletchley, Milton Keynes,
MK1 1QR, UK

Authentic Books, PO Box 444
285 Lynnwood Avenue,
Tyrone, Georgia 30290-0444, USA.

Scripture quotations taken from the Holy Bible,
New International Version.

Printed and bound in India by OM Authentic Media,
Secunderabad - 500055, India,
email: printing@ombooks.org.

To Frieda,
my beloved life partner
and faithful co-worker
in our ministry
of equipping and encouraging
God's servants

CONTENTS

Preface

The seed thought for writing this book has its roots in the fertile soils of Tana Toraja, the homeland of the Torajanese people in the province of South Sulawesi, Indonesia. Frieda and I arrived in this isolated but stunningly picturesque, mountainous region in late 1968 together with our young family. As members of OMF International (formerly known as the Overseas Missionary Fellowship), we had been invited by the Toraja Protestant Church to assist with equipping their lay leaders.

However, life in Tana Toraja was more than just ministry. As important for us was our desire to make good friends with the local people. Doing this soon exposed us to the realities of living in a multireligious community.

One such reality we observed was how friendships among the youth group sometimes turned down 'love lane' and led through the door into a mixed-faith household. Not surprisingly a few of our Torajanese Christian friends were married to partners who espoused different religious beliefs.

Over the following twelve years we also lived in other regions of Indonesia. In each place, we met Christians married to non-Christians. We discovered that many Christians did not have clear answers for the question, 'May a Christian marry a person who comes from a different religious tradition?'

So began my own journey to hear what God says on this important question. I wanted to understand His will, not just from 'proof texts', but from the whole counsel of God.

I had a second concern on my heart as well. As a pastor and teacher, I wanted to communicate God's truth with love, understanding and sensitivity to the unique pressures of life in a multicultural, multifaith community.

We now reside in Australia. Twenty-first century Australia is a colourful mosaic of peoples with a wide diversity of cultures and religious traditions. The context for building friendships and relationships here, as in many other countries that have opened their doors to refugees and migrants, is almost identical to the multiethnic, multifaith context we experienced earlier in Indonesia.

That's the way it is in our modern world! For most of us, building relationships with people of contrasting religious beliefs has become a part of everyday life.

This applies to young people and also to their parents.

Christian parents face a new challenge of faith as they try to help their children in their choice of friends, finding that as the children grow older the parents have little control over that area of their lives. Often they discover that the beliefs, habits, languages and interests of their children's friends do not fit with the Christian standards and convictions that they have sought to instil in them.

How should Christian parents respond if they discover that one of their children is feeling romantically attracted to someone raised with vastly different religious beliefs and practices? Should they view these differences as a 'non-issue'? How would *you* respond in such a situation?

If we are true followers of Jesus, our responses should be determined not by personal or public opinion, but rather by what *God* says. From the very beginning of the Bible, we read that God is *for,* and not against, marriage and the forming of new families. After all, wasn't it God's idea in the first place to create us male and female?

This implies that the whole process of forming new families is a matter of highest priority and concern to God. It also means that we can expect to find in God's Word specific and definitive guidance for His people in choosing a marriage partner.

That's what I have aimed to share in this book—God's wisdom for His people as they form relationships with people from different faiths and diverse cultures.

Many people had a part in the preparation of this book. Early in my life God touched my heart and mind through the wise counsel of my Christian parents and other godly mentors.

Others in more recent years have shared their own marriage journeys, or given words of encouragement, or prayed diligently as I wrote. To each I am truly indebted and grateful.

One I'd like to mention is Dennis Wright, a former leader, colleague and friend with whom we served for nine years in Central Europe with Operation Mobilisation. Almost every time he wrote or every time we met, Dennis would ask, 'How's the book going?'

I'd also like to express my heartfelt appreciation to two OMF International colleagues and experienced editors: Fay Goddard, a retired OMF missionary, for her encouragement and assistance in the earlier stages; and Stephen McElroy, for his timely advice and hard work in the final stages. I am particularly indebted to Stephen for his expert and invaluable assistance in honing and clarifying the text and message of the book.

Without doubt my number one encourager and supporter has been, and still is, my own beloved life partner since June 1963—Frieda. Whenever I felt disheartened, doubting whether I should continue in this long and arduous task, Frieda had just the right word. Her wise counsel, her occasional gentle rebukes when I allowed myself to be pulled down by negative thoughts, and her sharp mind so ably editing and clarifying the text, was God's way of keeping me focused.

My own marriage has motivated me to write this book. Frieda and I have been blessed by God with oneness of heart and purpose, and with a rich and enduring love for each other.

I pray that many, including you, dear reader, will desire and earnestly seek after God's very best for your own marriage.

As you do, please read on!

Introduction

A story from England . . .

When Mahdi and Aida were married, they were both faithful to the religious traditions they had been taught since childhood. They lived busy working lives but also looked forward to becoming parents. However, after months of trying, Aida was still not pregnant. They were sad, and their families were extremely disappointed.

One day when she felt especially dejected, Aida met a friendly lady at the fruit and vegetable stand in their local supermarket. Seeing how troubled Aida looked, the lady asked her if everything was alright. Immediately Aida unburdened her heart. The lady answered by telling Aida that she knows Someone who could help her—Jesus. She asked Aida if she could pray to Jesus for her and ask Him if He would kindly give them a little baby. 'Of course,' she replied.

Six weeks later Aida missed her monthly period. Secretly and excitedly she made an appointment to see her doctor. Yes, the doctor confirmed, Aida was pregnant.

She could hardly wait to share the good news with her husband, although she was afraid to tell him the whole story.

Aida was in the supermarket some months later, already wearing maternity clothes, when she happened to meet the same kind lady. Aida's face glowed with joy as she told her friend the good news.

This friend then told her that Jesus wanted to do an even greater miracle for her—to give her His gift of peace. She left her phone number with Aida, adding that if ever she would like to have a chat, she should call her.

Aida often pondered this Christian lady's words in the following months while waiting for her baby to be born. She could sense a peace and beauty of life in this lady that she did not enjoy herself.

After Aida had given birth to a baby son, she decided to phone her friend and tell her the wonderful news. During their conversation, her friend said: 'I think we should thank Jesus for this precious miracle, don't you agree?' Such a thought had never entered Aida's mind because she only prayed formal prayers to God. Her friend encouraged her to thank Jesus for this miracle baby. She then added, 'Why not also ask Him for His gift of peace?'

She did, and a bigger miracle happened—the peace of God came into her heart. Later, when her husband returned home from work, he noticed something had changed. Aida decided to tell him the whole story.

That was three years ago. Aida still keeps in good contact with her special friend and, although Mahdi hasn't yet allowed her to attend her friend's church, he cannot deny that their baby is a miracle child. They are now expecting their second child.

➲➲➲

Prayer requests from Africa . . .

Pray for the women believers here. Many are fearful of meeting together, and there is only one woman leader. Most women are either divorced or living in households where their husbands have more than one wife. This includes the women in the church . . .

Pray for this woman leader, for her gifts to be used for the building up of the church. Her husband has strong religious convictions but now seems to be more open to the gospel. Pray that the Lord will get a hold of his heart and the hearts of his entire family.

We need prayer, too, for the families in the church. Only a few believing couples exist in the entire region. Pray for the Lord to bring the husbands of the believing wives into the church, and vice versa. Pray that the church would be built on the family principles which God would want for His church.

Pray also for the singles. Many say there are too few believers for them to marry another believer, so they are tempted to go outside the church to find a partner. Pray that the Holy Spirit would convict them not to do this, and instead to trust God to bring them the right partner according to His will.

➲➲➲

Concerns from Eastern Europe . . .

N. is really struggling at this time. She will turn thirty this year and for a woman in her country not to be married by thirty makes her socially abnormal. The good thing is that she shares openly about her struggles with some people, so this makes it easier for us to support her. But people like this are in a very vulnerable position and could easily fall into the trap of marrying a 'nice' non-believer. Often well-meaning church people make it even more difficult. Rather than being supportive, they just keep asking, 'When will you get married?'

➲➲➲

Honest confessions from Asia . . .

Dear Father, Mother, and younger brothers and sisters,

May this letter find you in good health, just as I am also enjoying good health. Thank you so much for your letter, which I received two months ago.

Father and Mother, I have something to tell you that is very hard for me to say. I told you on my last visit home at New Year's how difficult it was for me to attend church while working here. It would take most of my monthly salary to travel to the nearest city for Sunday services. Besides that, I don't know any other Christians there. I remind you of this so that you can better understand my constant loneliness since being placed here.

Well, something has happened. Yes, the news you heard is true. I know how shocked you must have felt to hear that I am now married, and now you know that it is not just a rumour.

But let me explain. One day my director introduced me to a young lady, making it clear that he expected me to agree that she should become my wife. Well, I can assure you that Esmat is a very nice girl. As you know, the traditions here are different from ours. One thing led to another until . . . well, until I had no other option. I had no choice. Yes, I had to change my religion to marry her. I couldn't even run away, because this position is my only hope for a prosperous future, and I know how important that is to you.

I will close now. The one who will deliver this letter will bring other news about my new family. Please forgive me for the great shame I have brought upon you and the whole family. I sincerely hope that you will not disown me, but in my heart of hearts I fear that this might happen.

Your son,
Peter

These stories paint vivid pictures of the real issues and struggles faced by Christians all around the world today. They may even be similar to your story, or to the experiences of others you know.

Such are the realities of the Christian life in our twenty-first century. How would God have us respond in such circumstances? What are our God-given responsibilities to each other in these matters?

If you are in the middle of the battle yourself—unsure about how to choose a life companion or anxious about the choice your family might make for you—you need God's help and encouragement.

Perhaps you are asking, 'How does God want me to respond to the expectations of my family and friends?' Or you may already be attracted to a non-Christian friend, thinking, 'This relationship feels so right'. Or you might be a puzzled parent, wondering how to help your son or daughter wrestling with similar issues and emotions.

Tough issues, aren't they? Does the Bible offer us practical answers in such painfully challenging situations? Yes, but not swift solutions! God gives us hope and encouragement for every difficulty no matter how hopeless it may appear. He gives counsel to His people who for varying reasons are facing the hard issues related to marrying a person of another religion.

This counsel—from God's inspired Word—constitutes the core message of this book. Part 1 addresses needs and situations faced by Christian singles. Part 2 grapples with some of the issues and challenges faced by Christian parents. Part 3 deals with special needs of Christians married to non-Christians. Throughout, it will be clear that the book is addressed to my fellow-believers, followers of our Lord Jesus Christ.

Finally, allow me to introduce my *persona* as the author of the letters and email messages you will read in the chapters ahead. You will soon discover that together with my wife, Frieda, I am working as an English language and literature university lecturer in a major city. I also lead a weekly Bible study group for students in our home and a small fellowship of believers close to the campus.

Another important part of my life is corresponding with my former students via email and letters. Most of them live and work in distant regional centres. Occasionally I correspond with their family or friends.

The first email message (Chapter 1) was written in response to a request from a final-year university student named Mark.[1] In it I offer advice on how he could or should respond to an unexpected request from a friend.

Note:

1 All names and email addresses in this book have been changed in order to protect the identity of the individuals concerned.

Section One

Letters to Singles

One

'Is Jamila God's Choice for Me?'

To: Mark@unisem.edu
From: Graham@KingJesus.net.au
Subject: God's choice for a wife

Hi Mark!

Thanks for your email. I'm so thankful that you found our recent conversation helpful. I also came away feeling encouraged, especially with your openness to God's ways.

However, our conversation about finding a suitable life partner seems to have sent you off into orbit! I understand why you are finding it hard to concentrate on your studies! But with your final exams and graduation on the horizon . . . Sorry for the reminder but it would be wise to study, don't you agree?

Obviously, what has most hindered your studies has been receiving Jamila's 'love letter'. And to think that it arrived right after our conversation on that very topic. So Jamila thinks you are a special guy, does she? I agree with her opinion of course!

Your question is a good one: 'Is Jamila God's choice for me?' I feel honoured to have this special opportunity to think and pray with you for God's direction in this most important issue of your life. Here are some thoughts for your prayer and reflection.

I too found myself asking: Could this attractive young woman be God's choice for my friend Mark? I've also been reflecting on a related question: Has God in fact promised that *He* will choose a life partner for us?

Fascinating questions, aren't they? In our desire to walk in God's ways, these are questions we need to wrestle with. The good news is that God Himself has promised to guide us as we search for His way.[1] How much harder if we were forced to trust in man's wisdom!

So, what are God's answers? The more I study God's Word, the more I discover that truth often has two equally true dimensions. Yes, God has a plan for your life, but He also gives you the privilege and responsibility to make the choice yourself.

Is that confusing? I hope not. Some people might argue that if God chooses, then He can't also leave the choice with us. But there is no contradiction here. For example, think of God's gift of salvation. On the one hand, the Bible teaches us that we belong to God by His will, not by chance or by our own human will. But the Bible also says that it is our responsibility to turn to God from our old way of living and from our unbelief, in order to accept His free gift of eternal life.[2] Both are equally true.

So God's answers are: 'Yes', and 'yes'! Yes, He has mapped out your entire life, Mark, and yes, He invites you to join with Him in the decision-making process. This means that your desire to find a godly wife has been on the Father's heart a very long time! Even before you were born, Mark.

This is such good news, because it tells you that God is personally and intimately interested and involved in every area of your life, including this process of finding a suitable life partner. Yes, you will make the final choice, but you may ask your heavenly Father to direct your footsteps so that you do not stumble or fall.[3] Be confident that as you seek to know His mind and plans for your life, these will be *good* plans, plans that will fill your life with good things.[4]

Well, I'm already anticipating your next question: If this is true, *how* will God guide me in deciding whether or not Jamila is His choice for me? God knows we have questions like this. In response, he gives us two sources of divine guidance: His Word, the Bible, to instruct and guide us as we seek to understand His will, and His Spirit to help us understand and apply His Word to the particular challenges in our lives. Mark, as you look for direction in God's Word and ask for the help of God's Spirit, I know you will make a wise decision.

'Could Jamila be God's choice of a life's partner for me?' God answers your question in a wide variety of Scriptures, but the best point to begin your search is at the very beginning of His Book.

In the opening chapters of Genesis, among all the thrilling accounts of creation, God tells us how He first introduced Adam to his wife, Eve. Eve didn't pin a 'love letter' on a tree for Adam to read! In fact, Eve wasn't even around yet to share the Garden of Eden with Adam. Poor Adam was alone.

But God saw Adam's special need and had a way to meet it.[5] He planned for Adam a most beautiful life companion and partner. Like him, she would be created in God's image and would perfectly complement him—physically and on every other level of life and relationship. So God made Eve and brought her to Adam so they could share their life and work according to God's plan. How thrilled Adam must have felt when he first saw Eve!

Then God's Word makes an important statement: *'For this reason a man will leave his father and mother and be united to his wife, and they will become one flesh.'*[6] God gave us this Scripture in order to guide His people to a true understanding of His purpose in marriage. I believe this Scripture is God's word of wisdom that will guide you in responding to Jamila's letter.

Let's take special note of the phrase: *'... and be united to his wife.'* God's design for marriage is that we experience and enjoy genuine unity or *oneness* between husband and wife. Yes, even in some Christian marriages we see disunity and disharmony. However, man's failure doesn't alter God's plan since the beginning: man and woman, living in complete unity.

If you were to choose Jamila as your wife, would you be able to become truly 'one' in marriage? (I realize that at this stage, she's just written a love letter to you—but let's not pretend as if there's no idea in her mind about marriage!) 'One in marriage'—that's the hard part, isn't it? Jamila, though a fine young woman, is not a follower of Jesus.

Although, as you told me, she and her family are not strict about their religious beliefs, in God's sight the real issue is: Could you experience true oneness with a person who has not yet embraced the gospel of our Lord Jesus? You could become one on some levels, but at the very core of your being and relationship—on the level of the spirit—you could not enjoy the one mind, one heart and one purpose which God designed for marriage.

This I believe is *God's* answer to your question, Mark. It may not have been the answer you had hoped to hear but it is the answer that you need to hear. Though Jamila is intelligent and pretty with an outgoing personality, she and you are not 'one in Christ'. That alone is the 'glue' that would truly cement your relationship. Mark, my dear friend, please don't aim at anything less than God's best!

The choice is now yours. But knowing you, I'm confident that you will say 'yes' to God's higher plan. Please don't worry about the future. God understands your need to share and manage life together with someone with whom you can truly be one—especially on the level of the spirit. He has this part of your life in His hands—and in His heart.

I've already been praying to God about this need in your life, and I will continue to pray. I'll now pray about your immediate need to give a thoughtful and kind response to

Jamila. Let's also pray for Jamila herself, that God will speak to her through your words.

When then can we spend another hour or two together? Would you be free this Thursday evening? Until then, don't forget to study!

Your friend and fellow-pilgrim,

Graham

Notes:

[1] Psalm 32:8, 9

[2] John 1:12, 13

[3] Jude 24, 25

[4] Jeremiah 29:11

[5] Genesis 2:18

[6] Genesis 2:24; Matthew 19:5; Ephesians 5:31

Two

God Understands and Cares

Dear Sarah,

Your letter arrived this morning. It was good to hear from you again, and I was especially encouraged to read of your continuing prayers for our work among the students and faculty in this strategic campus. Thank you Sarah, and thank You God, for hearing Sarah's prayers!

Even though it's been two years since your graduation, God continues to use the witness of your life in the student body and also among some of the faculty. Just the other day, the unforgettable Dr. Steinfeld mentioned your name very warmly while chatting with me in the staff lounge.

From your letter, it's clear that you need encouragement. Thanks for sharing the news of your parents' insistence that you accept their choice of a future husband. I know how much you respect them, so it must have been very difficult to say no.

I could also sense your pain: 'But I see no one else on the horizon!' I was glad, however, that you could also say, 'Nevertheless I know that God, who is full of kindness and love, understands the burdens of my heart and will care for all my needs'.

Of course, this doesn't stop the tears as your family and friends continually question and criticize you. Nor does it stop you from becoming angry and frustrated as they pressure you to give in and accept their plan.

I'm sure they must be questioning why you are rejecting their 'perfect choice' of a future husband. Obviously their idea of an ideal husband is in radical contrast to your own convictions, based on God's Word, about who you as a believer should marry.[1]

Sarah, these emotions and struggles are normal. So don't think of yourself as a weak Christian because you aren't always feeling on top of the world. God doesn't condemn you for feeling this way—He knows we are all weak![2] For this very reason He tells us to cast our burdens on to Him, promising to sustain and strengthen us so we can cope with the pressures of life.[3] Through His help you will even grow, spiritually and emotionally, in this pressure-packed environment.

What most impressed me in your letter was your longing for a husband who is a *true* believer, a man of God whom you could respect as your spiritual leader and to whom you could joyfully and confidently submit.[4] I was also impressed by your insight: 'How can I accept a man to become my husband if he does not know or submit to the spiritual authority of Christ?'

But now you feel caught. You want to obey God's Word to respect and obey your parents,[5] yet also to honour His command not to marry someone who does not share your trust in our Lord Jesus Christ.[6]

It's difficult to reconcile these two commands, isn't it? Does God's Word contradict itself? We know that this is impossible. Why? Because God is ONE,[7] which means that each part of His truth will always be in perfect agreement and unity with every other part.

While God commands you to respect and obey your parents, He also declares that He Himself is your highest Authority, above all human authority figures.

Thus your principal duty is to submit to *His* will, even when it is in conflict with the wishes of your parents.[8] Of course, I am writing this counsel to a mature Christian woman in her mid-twenties, not to a young child. Furthermore, even if God's will for you means that you cannot accept your parents' choice of a husband, you must still obey God's command to *respect* your parents. I'm hoping that these few comments will help settle your concerns.

Your letter tells me that God has already been teaching you another of His commands—that when you marry, you are to love and submit to your husband, whom He has given to you as your spiritual leader.[9]

However, knowing and believing God's ways to be right and good do not stop us from having questions. So don't be astounded if you find yourself thinking, 'What am I doing? Here's an ideal opportunity to get married and I'm passing it by. Am I crazy?' Remember that God understands all your thoughts and feelings, and He loves you!

For moments like these, God has given us in His Word *many* words of encouragement.[10] I'll share one or two of these with you, praying that God's Spirit will deepen your conviction that you are indeed walking in His ways.

Dear Sarah, God's Word teaches that we have all been created by God in His own image.[11] One proof of this is our desire for relationships with other people.

You see, God is a relational God. How powerfully this is demonstrated within the Trinity. In the Gospels again and again we witness the pure and perfect relationship between Jesus, the Son of God, and His Father in heaven. Consider how Jesus spoke often about His delight to do His Father's will.[12] Think also of those beautiful, affirming words that the Father spoke to His Son at His baptism and transfiguration: *'You are my Son whom I love. With You I am well pleased.'*[13]

Clearly, God delights in relationships. He created us to have and to enjoy our human relationships, including the most intimate one of all—marriage. So He already knows this special need in your life.

But above all, He has made us to enjoy an intimate and everlasting relationship *with Himself*. This is expressed so powerfully in St. Augustine of Hippo's *Confessions:* 'You have made us for Yourself, O God, and our hearts are restless till they rest in You.'

I know your heart resonates with this wonderful declaration. Yet sometimes we hope that people will satisfy our deepest relational needs, which only God can meet. Many Christians enter into marriage expecting that they will find the ultimate intimacy there. Inevitably such false expectations lead to disappointment and disillusionment.

But if you make your relationship with *God* the number-one love relationship,[14] doesn't that mean that you can only hope for second-rate intimacy in marriage? The truth is just the opposite. As we draw closer to God, not only does this intimacy deepen and enrich our love relationship with Him, it also strengthens our relationship with our believing husband or wife.

Sarah, I pray that what I have just shared with you will inject a fresh sense of hope and trust in the true and living God. He created you to enjoy intimacy on every level of relationship, both with Himself and with others—especially the man who will one day become your life partner.

So please keep praying for that man of God for whom your heart desires. Trust God to bless you with this very special gift. God will fulfil His holy purposes in your life for the glory of His name and also for your pleasure and enjoyment.

Dear Sarah, we love you and are standing with you in prayer throughout this tough testing time in your life. We hope you will find a free moment to write to us again. We'd also love to hear how your new job is working out and also a little news about your church family.

With our warm and affectionate greetings.

Your brother in God's family

Graham

Notes:

[1] 1 Corinthians 9:5
[2] Psalm 103:13,14
[3] Psalm 55:22
[4] Ephesians 5:23, 24
[5] Compare Ephesians 5:23, 24 with Ephesians 6:1-3
[6] 2 Corinthians 6:14, 15
[7] Deuteronomy 6:4
[8] Acts 4:19, 20; 5:29
[9] Colossians 3:18
[10] 2 Corinthians 1:3, 4; 2 Thessalonians 2:16, 17
[11] Genesis 1:26, 27
[12] John 4:34; 5:19, 20a
[13] Luke 3:22
[14] Deuteronomy 6:5; Matthew 22:37-40; John 13:34, 35; 14:21; Revelation 2: 4,5

Three

The Greatest Treasure

Dear Joshua,

How are you doing, my good friend? From the news that has reached us by the grapevine, I guess you would say 'Fantastic!' Yes, Maria phoned to tell me about your intention to marry your former university classmate Fatima.

Now I understand why we haven't heard from you! Don't imagine that we haven't been thinking of you or praying for you. How could we? Ever since you came into our lives during your student days—didn't we have some great times together?—we have often mentioned your name in our prayers.

Let me tell you honestly our greatest prayer for you: that God would make your faith in Jesus come alive. Why this prayer? Because we love you, and long that your faith in Jesus will advance from just attending church and Bible studies to a living faith that impacts every area of your life.

Joshua, I must also be honest and say how surprised and sad we were on hearing of your marriage plan. But this doesn't change our great affection for you. Please don't imagine that our lack of excitement is a sign that we don't care for you or aren't interested in continuing our friendship.

Nor are we negative towards Fatima. In fact, my memories of her as a student are positive—even humorous, as I remember how she would eat peanuts during my lectures (somewhat noisily!). I spoke to her about this 'interesting' habit, but she politely explained that she needed this extra energy to keep awake and focused in my afternoon lectures!

So then, Joshua, why are we concerned about your intention to marry her? I'm sure you know! To begin with, Fatima is not a follower of Jesus—or at least not yet. Of equal concern to us is that it appears you are bowing to her parents' wishes that you change your religion in order to have Fatima as your prize. Of course it's not surprising that her father, as a prominent government official, would insist that you change your religion if you want to marry his daughter.

Yet I'm shocked to hear such news. I've been pondering how you could have reached this decision. I wonder if you've been thinking something like this: 'I won't give up my Christian beliefs. I'll hold on to them in my heart. I'll just go along with whatever is expected of me and see how things work out.'

But Joshua, no one can believe in Jesus and at the same time deny Him through his confession of faith and how he lives. Allow me to appeal to your sharp, logical mind to recognize that this strategy is totally unreasonable and unworkable. Above all else, it's unacceptable to God.[1] You cannot play word games with God. No one can fool Him,[2] for He knows even the secret thoughts and motives of our hearts.[3]

I pray that you examine your heart honestly before God. Ask yourself: 'What is my motivation in wanting Fatima for my wife?' Could there be hidden reasons? No doubt you've been attracted by her intelligence and beauty, but could it also be that you've been drawn by her family's wealth and influence?

I'm thinking of another possibility—that Fatima's parents have seen in you positive character qualities that cause them to wish for such a man of worth to become their daughter's husband. In fact, I'm almost sure that this is a major piece in the bigger puzzle. This is a wonderful compliment for you, and also for your Christian faith.

However, if in winning Fatima as your prize you must forfeit another of far greater worth, is that a good exchange? I hope you know which other prize I'm referring to—Jesus.[4] He is infinitely more precious than any other treasure you will ever find in this world.[5]

It may seem that changing your religion is a simple matter of going through a brief ritual. If that's the case, then it can only mean that the Good News of Jesus Christ has never moved from your head into your heart—from being mere head knowledge to becoming a living faith that flows out from the centre of your being into every area and choice of your life.

But, Joshua, finding Christ as life's ultimate treasure is at the core of our Christian faith. Anyone who finds this Treasure is changed forever.[6] It's only when you grasp this that you will understand why I say it's unthinkable to give away this Treasure for a human treasure—even a wife like Fatima.

You are at a crossroads, Joshua. Jesus is standing there calling you to follow Him. I believe that God has allowed you to come to this crossroad experience so that you might gain once and for all this living faith in His Son. With all my heart, dear friend, I urge you to listen to and receive Jesus' call.[7]

Please don't imagine as I write these things to you that I'm unaware of the difficulty and challenges of making this choice. Jesus never promised that following Him would be easy.[8] However, if you open your heart wide to His call, God will open your eyes to see the beauty and richness of Jesus as life's highest Treasure. And with this renewed vision of Jesus, you will have a completely different outlook on any short-term loss, even the possible loss of a potential beautiful bride.

So this is the challenge I set before you. Fix your eyes on Jesus. If you do, I can promise you all the other treasures hidden in Christ.[9] Including a believing wife? Of this I'm sure—God delights in giving good gifts to His people, and one of His very best gifts is a believing life partner. So do not be afraid to ask Him for this blessing (and many others).

Could God even use your commitment to Jesus to awaken within Fatima and her parents a longing to inherit this same Treasure? That may seem like a dream right now. But nothing is impossible with God!

Yet if you waver and turn down a different path, be sure that your losses will be far, far greater—both in this life and in the life to come.

Joshua, my dear friend, believe me—you are much in our hearts these days and in our prayers. Please don't hesitate to contact me if you would like to chat further about any of the issues I've raised in this letter. I'd be only too willing to phone you one evening if that would be convenient. I'll be anxiously waiting to hear from you.

Yours affectionately,

Graham

Notes:

[1] Romans 10:9, 10
[2] Galatians 6:7a
[3] Hebrews 4:13; Psalm 139:1-4
[4] Philippians 3:14
[5] Matthew 13:44-46; Philippians 3:7, 8
[6] Acts 9:1-22; 26:1-19; 2 Corinthians 5:17
[7] Matthew 11:28
[8] Luke 9:23-25; 18:18-23
[9] Colossians 2:2, 3, 9, 10

FOUR

GOD BLESS THIS FRIENDSHIP?

Dear James,

I was very happy to find your letter in my post box last week. Thank you for your kind words concerning our friendship, which means a lot to me too. Although we are unable see each other often while you are working in the interior, we can still write.

I was happy to hear your news, particularly that you have found a small group of fellow-believers. God's Word encourages us to journey side by side in our spiritual walk (I'm sure you remember our campus Bible studies) so we don't lose heart.[1] That's especially important when we encounter opposition to our faith—something that is hardly foreign to you in your present location!

James, thanks for your trust in telling me about your friend Premala and for being honest about her religious background. I was glad to read that you do not want to rush into a romantic relationship with her. But let's be honest—most of us find it hard to keep such emotions under check. Am I right?

However, praise God that Premala has already attended one of your fellowship meetings, and for the warm welcome she received from the sisters.

You asked us to pray for God's blessing upon your friendship with Premala. To pray for a blessing is not difficult, nor is it a hard prayer for God to answer! So you may be confident that Frieda and I will ask for His blessings upon your friendship.

How may we expect God to answer this prayer? Can we be sure that He is interested in blessing our friendships? Yes we can—and not sparingly, but *abundantly*![2]

But *how* He blesses, and with what *kind* of blessing, is His prerogative. The main thing we need to know is that God's blessings will always be good, never harmful.[3]

Even so, the way He answers may sometimes confuse or disappoint us. But if we sincerely want to welcome God's blessings, no matter how He chooses to bless us, each and every blessing will enrich us spiritually.[4]

So you should be prepared if God's answer to our prayer about your friendship with Premala is different than what you expected. Let me illustrate what I mean from my own spiritual journey. When I was a student in training for the Christian ministry, I often prayed asking God to use me to bless many people. In my mind, I expected that He would answer this prayer by making me a renowned evangelist among my own people in Australia. But instead He sent us to a remote region in Indonesia to teach His people to know Christ, to live for Him and to become effective witnesses for Him among their own people.

I soon came to realize that God's plan was right for me. He knew me far better than I knew myself. As a result, not only did we thoroughly enjoy living among the Torajas, but through our lives and ministries, He blessed many of His people in that corner of His earth.

Whatever God's answer, I hope you will be able to respond in trust: 'Father, although right now I cannot understand all Your ways, I welcome Your blessings, trusting in Your kindness and goodness.'

Remember too that God's blessings will always fit perfectly with His higher plan for your life, and also with Premala's. You can be sure that this includes His plan to bless you with a strong, happy marriage.

But James, God's desire to bless you goes beyond this. You see, when God pours out His blessings upon us believers, He intends that these gifts of blessing will also enrich the lives of many, including those who do not yet know Him as their Lord and God[5]—like Premala.

Sometimes, however, we forget this aspect as we ask for God's blessings. Even as Christians, our thoughts can fall prey to the subtle influence of self-interest and self-importance. We may make a very good-sounding request to God—including the blessing of a friendship—which in fact is self-centred. We want only what will make us happy and content.

By now it will be obvious to you that our praying for

God's blessing upon your friendship with Premala is more than just offering up a prayer to God. Even before praying, we must ask God to expose any hidden motives that might work against His plan to bless.

James, I know your heart—both your longing after God, and also your longing for a beautiful human relationship. Keep focused on God's higher purposes in your life.[6] Be continually alert to Satan's intent to direct your thoughts away from *God's* best to what *you* think is best. Ask God to cleanse you from anything contrary to His holy will—things that will bring sadness instead of God's joy into your life.[7]

Make sure that the number-one passion in your heart and in your prayers is to please Jesus your Master and to fulfil His purposes in your life[8]—including His purpose for a marriage that will be a blessing to others.

How should this be reflected in your prayers for Premala? Obviously in praying for her we desire God to give Premala the greatest spiritual blessing of all—the blessing of an eternal relationship with Himself, of knowing that all her sins have been forgiven through Jesus' sacrifice on the cross.[9]

Of course you and I don't know how or when God will answer this prayer. So until she opens her heart to Jesus (we hope that will be soon!), how should you relate with her? Should you nurture the friendship? Should you break it off?

I have three suggestions. First, keep your friendship with Premala as a normal, everyday friendship until she is a genuine believer.[10] Don't allow it to become a romantic relationship—yet! I'm not urging you to suddenly turn cold and unfriendly towards Premala. Of course not! Be your usual friendly self, but avoid any physical touch and romantic talk with her.

Second, find an appropriate opportunity to talk with Premala. She already knows that you are a Christian. It's now time to take the next step and share your faith in Jesus. She needs to know that your friendship with Jesus is the number-one relationship in your life—and the relationship that she must also experience before you are willing to develop a closer friendship with her. However, say this with kindness and gentleness so that Premala doesn't feel that she must make a quick or superficial decision.

Third, ask God to show you creative ways to stir within Premala a desire to personally experience God's wonderful salvation in Jesus. Probably it would be best if one or two sisters in your fellowship could establish a friendship with Premala. Then pray, asking God to bless their friendship with her so that if it is pleasing to Him, you may later have her as *your* special friend.

James, wouldn't it be exciting for you if our heavenly Father answered these prayers tomorrow? Still, let's set our hearts on waiting patiently for God to finish His saving work in Premala before making any other plans.

Even if God were to answer your prayer immediately, I'm sure that you see the wisdom in not rushing quickly into a romantic relationship. Give Premala time to enjoy the wonders of her love relationship with Jesus, before you turn your sights to developing a love relationship with her.

My dear friend James, yes, I will pray for God's blessing upon your friendship with Premala as you have asked—and as God Himself desires to bless your friendship for *His* glory and according to *His* higher plans.

For your part, remain committed always to pleasing and honouring Jesus no matter how God answers your prayers.

Your brother in God's great family,

Graham

Notes:

[1] Hebrews 10:23-25

[2] Psalms 65:11; 103:11, 17

[3] Psalm 84:11, 12

[4] Ephesians 1:3, 7, 8; Proverbs 10:22

[5] Psalm 67; Genesis 18:18

[6] Isaiah 55:8, 9

[7] Psalms 51:10; 139:23, 24

[8] Romans 12:1; 2 Corinthians 5:9

[9] Ephesians 1:7

[10] 2 Corinthians 6:14, 15

FIVE

NOT A VICTIM OF FATE

My dear sister Joanna,

Today your friend Naomi stopped by our home to deliver your note telling us that your parents and family have set the wedding date. I'm hoping that Naomi will soon return to you with this letter reminding you of the love and support of all your Christian brothers and sisters here. Please know that we remain fully committed to you.

We can only imagine how stressful the recent weeks have been, with mounting pressure on you to agree with their plan for you to marry Akbar. Don't ever think that we blame you for finally agreeing to your parents' wishes. From your note, it's clear that you were given no choice.

Joanna, please know that you are so very dear to each of us. From the first day you became a part of our fellowship—in your final year of studies—we have been so thankful to see God's mighty, life-changing work in you. Wasn't it a year ago this month when you and Naomi had your first conversation in the university cafeteria?

What an amazing thing God did that day. Naomi sensed the pain behind your politeness. How powerfully God cut through the barriers into your heart as she shared how God's love for you could replace your fear of His anger. Then you opened your heart to this Good News. I vividly recall your words: 'For the first time in my life, I saw God's indescribable beauty and glory reflected in His Son, Jesus.'[1]

That was indeed a day of wonderful beginnings for you. God is still turned towards you in compassion and love, even though you see dark events threatening to obscure the bright rays of His presence. Nothing, including your marriage to Akbar, can ever stop God from loving you.[2] Isn't that *good news*?

Maybe you can only say a faint 'amen' to this. I know that a devastating and unexpected trial can leave even the strongest believer reeling with doubts. It could be that you've been feeling a victim of fate, as if everyone and everything is against you.

I too have experienced valleys in my Christian life. I've even wondered, does God really answer prayer? Please don't allow the evil one to tempt you into thinking that God has turned His face away from you in this difficult time.

If there's one message I want to communicate to you through this letter, it's this: You are *not* a victim of fate but the beloved child of a loving God. And because of His great love, He will overturn what now looks like very bad news so that it results in good news both for yourself and also for others. Let me prove this by telling you a Bible story where God turned a tragedy into a great triumph for His people.

Have you ever read the story of Esther in the Old Testament? It's a thrilling drama in which God brings life out of death, and hope out of a hopeless situation. Esther's story is so applicable to your present experience because she was also thrust into a marriage by circumstances outside her control.

Esther was a Jewess who lived about 480 years before Jesus was born. She was born and grew up in a foreign land far away from her people's homeland. Her family were exiles who had been subjected to the worst atrocities imaginable at the hands of cruel and fierce foreign soldiers.

Amid all the sadness of Esther's past was the sorrow she experienced at the loss of her parents. She was raised by her cousin, Mordecai, as his own child.[3] He undoutedly told her the stories of their nation's sufferings and how God had saved them from their enemies. As a young girl, Esther would have listened with rapt attention as Mordecai recited, for example, the story of God's divine rescue of the Jews from their Egyptian slave-masters under Moses' leadership.[4]

Her young mind had been shaped by such amazing demonstrations of God's power. She knew and believed that even in her people's darkest moments—when enemy nations had subdued and subjugated them—their God was able to rescue and redeem them.

Esther was a stunningly beautiful young woman and a true worshipper of God, the great Ruler of all nations. Though she was totally unaware of God's plan, He had foreordained her to play a primary role in yet another God-orchestrated plan to save His people from the hands of their enemies.

God Himself choreographed this drama on the world stage in Persia. Because Esther was so attractive physically, she drew the attention of the royal palace of King Xerxes, king of Persia, at a time when he was searching for a new queen.

She was brought into the king's palace along with other beautiful young girls, then prepared, through a long and rigorous treatment, with fragrant oils and lotions, to be presented to the king. I wonder if Esther thought, as the aromatic oils were massaged into her skin, *how is it possible that I, a believer in the one true God, could one day become the queen in this pagan Persian kingdom? Why is all this happening to me?*

Poor Esther! Outwardly she might have felt like a victim caught up in the wheel of fate—in a world in which an unbelieving king would have the final say. To make her situation even more confusing, her guardian, Mordecai, was supporting her involvement in this 'Miss Queen of Persia' beauty contest.

When Esther was finally escorted into King Xerxes' presence, did she expect to be the one chosen as King Xerxes' new queen? Clearly she did not know that God's hand had been guiding all the events in the king's palace in order to rescue His people.

As the story unfolds, we discover that God had a special calling for Esther beyond her farthest expectations. He would use her influential and intimate contact with the king in order to deliver His people from a vile plot to exterminate all Jews in the Persian kingdom. Over the coming weeks, God accomplished this plan through Esther's willing, skilful and potentially life-threatening intervention before the king.

Dear Joanna, do you believe that Esther's God is also your God? I know you do. Though you are still puzzled as you try to understand why God did not stop your parent's plan, you can be certain that He is at work weaving into the tapestry of your life a far more beautiful pattern than any of us can see now.[5]

This won't mean that each day of your marriage will be smooth-sailing. However, we your Christian family here will keep supporting you in prayer, asking God to keep your faith alive and strong, whether your days be dark and dreary or bright and cheery.

And we will also be praying for Akbar, joining our faith with yours as we ask God to pour out His grace upon him through your life,[6] and then later through the children God will entrust to you both.

We'll have you in our thoughts and prayers as you prepare for the various wedding rituals and ceremonies. We know that the rituals could be a spiritual struggle for you. But God is greater and more powerful than all the forces of darkness.[7] Our faithful Lord Jesus, who is within you, dear Joanna, will watch over you to foil any of Satan's evil designs to gain access to your spirit.[8]

So may God's peace garrison your mind and rule over your thoughts and your words so that your life—both on the wedding day and every succeeding day—is a living testimony to the power of God's grace and love at work in your life. May

Akbar himself see and be drawn to put his trust in such a wonderful Saviour, our Lord Jesus Christ.

My final word to you, dear Joanna, is this: every time you hear 'fate' whispering in your ear, respond with conviction: 'No, neither fate nor man's will is in control of my life, but my loving God. I have given over the controls of my life to Him. I have nothing to fear.'

Standing strong with you, our dear sister,
Your brother in God's precious family,

Graham

Notes:

[1] John 1:14, 18; 2 Corinthians 4:6; Hebrews 1:1-3
[2] Romans 8:35-39; Psalms 34:15; 103:8-12
[3] Esther 2:7
[4] Exodus 15:1-21
[5] Romans 8:28-30
[6] 1 Corinthians 7:13, 14
[7] 1 John 4:4; 2 Corinthians 10:3-5
[8] John 14:18-20

SIX

ASHAMED... AND FORGIVEN

Dear Rachel,

Your letter took much longer than usual to reach me, but the important thing is that it made it.

How painful it must have been to write such a letter! 'Hardly an hour goes by without something that stirs the memory of that evening by the beach. Why was I so foolish? I liked Arjun as a friend but I had nothing more in my mind. And now I'm pregnant. My life is in ruins.'

We are so thankful that you were brave enough to tell us this news yourself. After reading it, Frieda and I paused and prayed for you. I pray now that God will comfort and encourage you through this letter.

Before I say anything else, please be sure of one thing: You are still our dear sister in Christ—a precious, dearly loved child of God, one of us![1] So please stop wondering if we would ever want to see you again. If only you could visit us right now!

More important, our Father in heaven hasn't turned His face away from you.

Dear Rachel, don't keep mulling over the past; that will only lead to despair. It's time to seek God's help for the future. Looking through God's eyes will lighten your burdens and give you fresh hope.

I commend you for your honesty, admitting that you sent wrong messages to Arjun through your physical contact with him. On the other hand, I also sense that your focus is still inward. That's an important part of your journey towards recovery and healing, but now it's time to think of how *God* sees your sexual encounter with Arjun.

This is the most important issue, even more than your feelings of shame and distress as you face the consequences of that evening.

The Bible tells us that whenever we sin, whether secretly or with another person, we are sinning against *God*.[2] Acknowledging this is the starting point in your journey towards spiritual healing—putting on God's attitude, realizing that you disobeyed His holy law.

But that is just one side of the coin. The other side is equally important—God's mercy. Rachel, His greatest delight and desire is to forgive you, not to judge and condemn you.[3] Isn't that wonderful news?

You needn't fear that God will punish or get even with you because of your sin. Our God will not do that. Nor can He, because He already poured out His wrath for all our sins upon Jesus. The day Jesus was crucified was the day of our salvation because all our sins, including your sin with Arjun, were nailed to His cross.[4]

Dear Rachel, for this very reason God can now pour out His mercy upon you, offering you full and free pardon instead of eternal judgement[5]. Can we ever comprehend such unbelievable kindness?

Your part then is to respond in faith to God's marvellous act of mercy. He calls to you: 'Come to Me, My beloved child. Hand over all your feelings of shame. All I ask is that you confess your sin to Me and receive the Good News of My Son's death and resurrection as My gift for you.'[6]

If you can, find a quiet place as soon as you finish reading this letter and welcome God's mercy and grace into your heart. (Writing this encourages me, because I need His forgiving grace too—we all sin against God.)

One other comment before I address the main question in your letter. Rachel, expect that Satan will keep attacking you with feelings of shame and hopelessness. He will accuse you of failure.[7]

Our struggle is that we often mistake the voice of the devil for the voice of God's Spirit. We hear Satan's accusations and condemn ourselves, falling prey to dark thoughts and dismal feelings of unworthiness. How can we distinguish between these opposing voices? Rachel, the voice that depreciates or corrupts your view of God's glory and keeps you focused on His anger is the voice of the enemy. The voice that reveals and calls you to confess your sin so that you may be forgiven is the voice of God.[8]

Silence Satan by reminding him who you are—God's child,

whose sins were banished from His sight through Jesus' sacrifice on the cross.[9] Rachel, it doesn't matter how often in a day you need God's grace to comfort your heart. His grace is always greater than your sin.

Satan may also attack us through our relationships. I was sad to learn that your parents reacted so strongly when you told them you were pregnant. But their reaction is understandable, don't you agree? They probably feel ashamed and angry because they fear they will lose all they have sacrificed in order to give you a university education.

Please give them time to work through these feelings. I hope that as fellow-Christians they will accept your apology and forgive you. (I spoke with your parents a few days ago. I phoned them because I wanted them to know that we also feel their sadness. Don't forget to pray for them, too.)

Now to the big question: 'Should I accept the proposal of Arjun and his family that we get married?' This is not an easy question to answer. However, my simple answer is no. I do not find any instruction in the Scriptures that commands a woman to marry a man who has made her pregnant.

Added to this is the fact that Arjun is not a follower of Jesus. God clearly commands us in the Bible *not* to marry a person who does not believe in Jesus Christ, as his one and only Saviour and Lord.

To understand God's mind on this matter, study Exodus 34:14-16, Deuteronomy 7:1-4 and 2 Corinthians 6:14-18. The Bible has much more to say on this topic. Please ask if you're interested in studying it in greater depth.[10]

I trust you won't mind if I raise another practical issue: Does God want you to say anything to Arjun about that evening? Dear Rachel, it's very humbling, but yes, God teaches us when we sin against someone, to confess our sin to that person.[11]

Please don't misunderstand. God does not expect you to accept full responsibility for what happened. All He asks is that you admit your part and ask Arjun to forgive you. Of course, his attitude towards what happened that night will be very different to yours. He may have even planned the evening with that outcome. If so, that's his responsibility. You just need to be honest about your part, as you were in your letter to us.

How should you say this to him? Speaking face to face would be ideal—if you can. If that would be too difficult for you, you could write him a brief note. Go straight to the point. Admit your part in the sin, without preaching at Arjun or accusing him. Then close by thanking God that He is willing to forgive you.

Who knows, God could use your confession as a Gospel moment in Arjun's life. Your humbling yourself may at first seem ridiculous to him, but in God's hands it could touch his heart.

What would the Lord have you do about the life that is now growing within you?[12] As Creator of life, God hates all forms of destroying life, whether inside or outside the womb. He says this plainly in His Word,[13] so to abort this life would be to sin against God. Please don't listen to anyone who advises abortion. That would only lead to sadness and regret, guilt and shame.

What to do with this precious life is a very personal choice. It is your child, God's gift to you, despite the circumstances in which it was conceived. The choice you need to make is whether you will accept the responsibility of raising the child yourself or give that responsibility to another couple. Ask God to guide you and you will know what you should do.[14]

However, considering your present situation as well as your future, it may be wise to consider offering your baby up for adoption by a Christian couple or family. Without doubt you should speak with your parents, and also with your pastor, but the final decision will be yours.

If God leads you to offer your baby up for adoption by a Christian couple, that is a very responsible and loving act—responsible, because you are entrusting your baby's life into the care of people who will raise the child in a Christian way; loving, because you may be blessing a childless couple with the joy of becoming parents.

Above all, rest in the Lord's love and care for the child. He will always have His eye upon your child no matter in whose home he or she will be raised.

Let me tell you an amazing story we heard from a woman named Lee when she visited our church some years ago. Lee testified to God's awesome grace in the face of one of the greatest trials a woman can ever face.[15]

On the first day she started work, at seventeen years old, Lee was sexually assaulted by another employee. That was devastating enough, but she was shattered when she found out that she was pregnant. Her first thought was to have an abortion. Where she lived, abortions were common and easy to get. What's more, most people regarded it as the right solution for a rape victim.

But Lee's conscience wouldn't allow it, so she registered her pregnancy at an adoption agency, stipulating that her baby's adoptive parents must be true Christians. Over the following months, God worked one miracle after another, guiding the adoption agency in choosing a Christian couple for her child.

Lee gave birth to a beautiful baby girl. Immediately the baby was taken from her and given to her adoptive parents. After post partum recovery she returned to the routines of life and found a new employer.

The most astonishing miracle came many years later. As an adult, Lee's daughter one day decided she must find her birth mother. With the help of government agencies, she found Lee's phone number.

When Lee took the call she heard the voice of the daughter she had never known. 'I am phoning', she said, 'to tell you two wonderful things: firstly, that God loves you, and secondly, that you are now a grandmother!'

Do you believe that God can do miracles? This child from a rape had grown to become a mature Christian woman herself (with a Christian husband) and now had a baby of her own! Soon afterwards, grandmother, daughter and granddaughter met for the first time. Can you imagine how delighted God must have been as He witnessed their joy?

Dear Rachel, how great and awesome is our God! Truly

His power is far greater than our human minds could ever grasp,[16] and His grace far greater than even our greatest sin.

As I close this letter, I know that you have a lot to think and pray through in the coming weeks. Let me encourage you once more to focus your thoughts on the greatness of our glorious God: *'The LORD is compassionate and gracious, slow to anger, abounding in love. . . . For as high as the heavens are above the earth, so great is his love for those who fear him; as far as the east is from the west, so far has he removed our transgressions from us.'*[17]

With our love and frequent prayers for you, our dear sister.

Your brother in God's eternal family,

Graham

Notes:

1 Colossians 3:12
2 Psalm 51:4
3 Psalm 130
4 Colossians 2:13, 14
5 Ephesians 2:4, 5; Titus 3:4, 5
6 1 John 2:1, 2
7 Revelation 12:10; Romans 8:33, 34
8 1 John 1:9
9 John 1:29; Micah 7:18, 19
10 Genesis 26:34, 35; 27:46-28:2; Numbers 25:1-9; Deuteronomy 28:32; Joshua 23:11-13; Judges 13-16; 1 Kings 11:1-13; 16:29-33; 2 Kings 8:16-18, 25-27; Ezra 9:1-10:4; Nehemiah 13:23-27; Malachi 2:10-12; 1Corinthians 7:39; 9:5.

[11] James 5:16

[12] Psalm 139:13-16

[13] Exodus 20:13

[14] Psalm 32:8, 9

[15] The story of this Christian woman's testimony to God's grace is recorded in her book, *The Missing Piece*, by Lee Ezell (Ann Arbor, Michigan, USA: Servant Publications, 1992)

[16] Isaiah 55:8, 9; Romans 11:33

[17] Psalm 103:8, 11, 12

Seven

Beware! Danger Ahead

To: mattaboy@glowemail.org
From: Graham@KingJesus.net.au
Subject: Love & concern

Hi Matthew!

I'm sitting here thinking of that awesome farewell party we had for you eighteen months ago. It was an unforgettable evening!

What made it even more special was that you had just been offered that amazing I.T. job. We were so delighted—it was like a dream come true! Your graduation *cum laude* was well deserved, and your parents were so proud of you.

But now it looks like things have changed—and, I fear, not for the better. A couple of hours ago I awoke remembering the news we got yesterday from your big sister Elizabeth. That is why I'm up early writing this email.

Matt, my dear friend, my heart is profoundly troubled. I cannot believe that the Matt we knew, who was so alive spiritually during his university studies, is the same Matt who is now considering accepting the invitation of a beautiful colleague, a non-Christian woman, to live together.

Please tell me what is going on, Matt. Okay, it's a struggle being the only Christian in your office. But you are a follower of Jesus. Because of God's work within you, you are different and your lifestyle must also reflect your life in Christ.[1] You cannot follow Jesus and at the same time follow the standards of the crowd, who do not know Him.[2]

May I speak 'heart-to-heart'? Just imagine us sitting together in our living room sharing the struggles you've been going through—complete with a cup of your favourite coffee!

As a follower of our Lord Jesus Christ, you are no longer in charge of your choices, your work or your relationships. You might have a sharp mind, an A-1 body, a lively personality and a good-paying job. But these aren't your personal possessions, they are God's.

If you forget this, Satan can turn your natural abilities into spiritual liabilities. Do you remember what I said the day before your graduation last year? 'Above all, guard you heart lest the enemy puff you up with pride.'[3] If that were to happen you would be vulnerable to all kinds of other dangers.

We had no idea then what would happen after you started this job. But we knew Satan's ways—and that this great deceiver can devise cunning ways to tempt us. We knew that you must resist him,[4] and that's what you must do now.

No doubt the offer from your friend is attractive. But Satan loves to twist the good things of God, including our sexual passions, for destructive purposes. He wants to wreck your life!

There's only one way to respond and that is to *run* for your life.[5] This is exactly what the Old Testament character Joseph did when a woman of influence tried to entice him into bed with her.[6]

Like you, Joseph was a gifted, intelligent and good-looking young man. One day his older brothers, out of jealousy, sold him to slave-traders on their way to Egypt.[7] Joseph suffered greatly at their hands, but faced an even greater trial after being assigned to work in the household of a leading Egyptian government official named Potiphar.[8]

Potiphar's wife became infatuated with this handsome Jewish slave and, with her husband away at work, thought Joseph would be easy game for some recreational sex. But Joseph had been raised to know and follow the ways of the living God. He knew that this woman's ways were contrary to the will of his God.

Again and again she tried to seduce Joseph, but he refused to give in. One day she decided to 'go for it' and tried physically to pull Joseph into her snare.[9] Joseph ran for his life, saving himself from grave moral danger—and from almost certain death if the tale of their affair had been leaked to Potiphar.[10]

I know you are familiar with Joseph's story, so you will remember the next part. The woman lied to her husband, shifting the blame and accusing their Hebrew slave of sexual misconduct. Her words and actions stand in stark contrast to the holiness of Joseph's God.

Joseph's integrity and faithfulness to God and His ways—passed on to him by his father, Jacob—resulted in his being shut away in a miserable Egyptian jail for two-plus years. But he was never shut away from God's favour.[11]

Another biblical character faced similar temptations, but responded very differently. Samson was also one of God's holy people, the Jews. Samson was given incredible strength to accomplish certain feats, but he did not share the strength of godly convictions which were so powerfully at work in Joseph's life.[12]

The path of Samson's life was darkened by a series of tragic moral failures. Though he believed in God, he married a Philistine woman, and the Philistines were enemies of God's people. Even the urgings of his parents failed to dissuade him from pursuing this disastrous downhill course.[13]

Yet God had the last word in Samson's life. Although Samson's weakness played into the hands of the Philistines, God kept His eye on him. He gave Samson supernatural strength in his dying moments to inflict a mighty defeat upon his enemies.[14]

Why do you think God allowed this tragic story to be recorded in the Bible? One reason undoubtedly was to warn us against mistakes that bring moral and spiritual ruin.[15]

Matt, I know you well enough. In your four years as a university student and an active participant in our church family we saw you as a young man who was passionate for God. I am convinced that you want to pattern your life after Joseph's life, not Samson's. That is what God wants.

I plead with you: Embrace God's holy desires for you, and fight against the evil designs of our enemy. God wants you to wait until you marry a woman after His own heart. He has wonderful pleasures in store for you through Christian marriage. Don't throw that all away. Instead, throw away this plan of living together. All of us—including Elizabeth and all your Christian brothers and sisters here—urge you to stop before it's too late. Take decisive action, Matt, and tell your friend that as a Christian, you cannot accept her invitation.[16]

I also urge you to cut all romantic links with her.[17] That could lead to ridicule and rejection in the office, even false rumours. But by following God's will, like Joseph you will enjoy God's favour.[18]

Even if you had to resign or ask for a transfer, would that matter? If your work environment threatens your spiritual and moral well-being, any other so-called benefits are worthless. Set your mind on eternal riches, even if this means temporary losses.

My dear friend and brother, please take my counsel seriously. All I've written to you flows out of love for you. You know that! I cannot bear to contemplate your moving away from our Lord Jesus, the One and only Source of true life.

One thing is for sure: We your Christian family will not

stop interceding for you. Please write me SOON telling me that you have received this email and have heeded my advice.

Your friend and brother,

Graham

Notes:

[1] Ephesians 4:17-24; 5:1-10
[2] 1 John 2:15-17; 2 Corinthians 6:14-18
[3] Proverbs 16:18; 1 Corinthians 8:1
[4] John 16:33; Matthew 6:13; James 4:7
[5] 1 Corinthians 6:18-20; 2 Timothy 2:22
[6] Joseph's story is found in Genesis 37-50
[7] Genesis 37
[8] Genesis 39
[9] Genesis 39:11-13
[10] Genesis 39:12
[11] Genesis 39:20, 21
[12] Judges 13-16
[13] Judges 14:1-3
[14] Judges 16:23-30
[15] 1Corinthians 10:11
[16] Proverbs 3:1-4; 5:1-14
[17] 2 Corinthians 6:14-18
[18] Psalm 1:1-3

Section Two

Letters to Parents

Eight
God at Work

Dear Paul and Mary,

Greetings in the holy name of Jesus Christ, our faithful Lord and Saviour.

Last week I was privileged to address a Christian youth leaders' training conference. After my talk I was approached by one of the delegates—a friend of yours, Karl Schmidt. He recognized my name in the programme. Apparently you've reminisced with Karl about your university years, including your fellowship with God's people here.

Right now I'm smiling, Paul. Do you remember the day when you fell asleep in one of my afternoon lectures and started snoring? And woke up when we all laughed? My apologies for a boring lecture!

Back to the youth leaders' conference . . . one afternoon Karl and I had coffee together. I was anxious to hear news about you. He was also anxious to tell me your news—first the good news about how much your friendship has meant to him, but then the sad news about Silas' recent marriage to Layla. I confess that this so deeply affected me that I was speechless.

Since then I've been looking for the right moment to share some words of encouragement. Even as I write I'm praying that God will use something you read in this letter to comfort and revive your spirits. I pray also that God will help you to hand all your cares and burdens to Him.[1]

You must be distraught. After faithfully raising Silas and your other children in the Christian way, how hard it must have been for you to witness your son marry a young woman who does not know the true God and Father of our Lord Jesus Christ.[2] I'm sure you've wondered, *How could Silas turn his back on us and the God we worship?*

Dear Mary and Paul, please don't let such thoughts rob you of your peace and trust in God. For one thing, you must not imagine that Silas has thrown his faith out of the window. Nor should you think that he has rejected you as his parents. After all, Karl told me that both he and Layla were anxious to involve you in their wedding rituals and ceremonies.

I commend you for doing so. Rather than reacting with hurt or bitterness on their day of celebration, you gave Layla and her family a striking example of Christian love in action.[3]

This morning I was meditating on Psalm 9. I thought of you when I read verse 10: *'Those who know your name will trust in you, for you, Lord, have never forsaken those who seek you.'*

Could God have given me this verse especially for you today? I believe so. I encourage you to write it down and place it where you can be frequently reminded of God's promise to you.

God gave me another experience that prepared me for writing this note. About a week ago a Christian brother stopped by for a visit. That he came at this time was surely planned by the Lord. Let me tell you why.

My friend, Ibrahim, grew up in a family and ethnic community traditionally opposed to the Christian faith. In contrast, his wife received a strong Christian upbringing. I asked him to tell me their story so I could retell it to you. So here goes!

Ibrahim met Ruth when they worked together in an office of the Public Works Department. As they discussed work matters, Ibrahim found her intelligent, friendly and fun-loving. Ruth has a good sense of humour—something most men enjoy, right?

Occasionally they discussed religious issues. Both held strong beliefs. Sometimes the atmosphere would become tense as one would try to change the other's point of view.

Their friendship turned a corner and they started talking about more personal matters. Ibrahim found himself more and more attracted towards her. He realized that the religious issue could create ill feelings between them, so he decided to stick with other topics when they met. He secretly believed that he would later succeed in winning her over to his side.

His strategy began to work. Ruth began thinking, *My*

relationship with Ibrahim is just like a dream come true. It must be God's answer to my prayers for a husband.

A couple of months later they decided it was time to tell their parents. Ibrahim's parents gave their enthusiastic support. They had already met Ruth a few times and had said to each other, 'She would make a very good wife for our son. It's about time he found a wife!'

When Ruth approached her parents, however, they were deeply concerned. With tears they pleaded with Ruth to immediately break off the relationship. Yet nothing they said would change her mind. Although they ultimately consented to the marriage, they continued to pray and hope for a change in their daughter's heart. The wedding day, when it finally came, was mingled with joy and sadness for Ruth's parents.

As the newlyweds began to settle into married life they continued to attend their own religious services. For Ruth this meant regular attendance at Sunday services and also at some home fellowship meetings.

Instead of winning her over to his side, Ibrahim admits that during this period he became increasingly impressed (secretly) with the Christian life of his wife and her parents.

As Ibrahim told his story, he shared with me the three main factors that ultimately won his heart to Jesus. *The first factor* was the steadfastness of his wife's faith. Previously he had viewed her Christianity as nothing more than a set of beliefs and rituals. In real life, he found himself living with a person whose faith in Jesus affected every part of her life—both in ordinary, everyday events, and also in suffering and disappointment. What most impressed him was the way she prayed openly to God.

One particular incident left an indelible impression on him. Ruth was experiencing a long and difficult labour before the birth of their second son, Omar. As the pain of her contractions grew more intense, Ruth cried out to God to have mercy on her and their little baby. God answered her prayers.

The second factor was how his parents-in-law welcomed him into their family circle. Because of his religious prejudices against Christians, at times he acted arrogantly towards them and made light of their Christian beliefs. However, their genuine affection for him left its mark on his spirit.

He was puzzled: *How can they remain warm and friendly to me when I've been rude to them? They never even appear to get offended.* In fact, sometimes they were quite hurt. But they chose not to allow their feelings to cause a rift between them and their daughter's family.

For eight long years, Ibrahim told me, Ruth's parents kept up their prayer vigil for Ibrahim and Ruth and their family. (By this time God had given them three children.) They prayed for Ruth and Ibrahim to become truly *one*, in spirit as well as in body.

And God was faithful. He answers prayer! Isn't that one of the foundations of our Christian faith? Although they saw no evidence of Ibrahim's attitudes softening, God was at work.

The climax to their prayers happened one day when Ibrahim and Ruth's oldest son, Arif, was struck down with an undiagnosed illness. This was *the third factor* in Ibrahim's journey towards Christ. With tears in his eyes, he told me how Arif's sickness almost resulted in his death. He and Ruth watched helplessly as their son slipped into unconsciousness. Even the doctors and hospital nursing staff were unable to arrest the infection that had gripped his young body.

Earlier that day Ruth had phoned her pastor hoping that he would come immediately to the hospital. But he was out of town, and his wife said he wasn't expected home until evening. His wife sent him an SMS message, asking him to go to the hospital as soon as he could.

It was nearly midnight when Ruth's pastor finally arrived at Arif's bedside. He found both mother and father desperate, crying uncontrollably beside Arif's listless body. The doctor had just told them that Arif's condition had turned critical.

Then God stepped in. Ibrahim said that his wife's pastor just prayed a very simple prayer in the name of Jesus, asking God to display His awesome power in healing this precious young life. And He did! By morning Arif had regained consciousness and by midday was asking for something to drink.

For days, Ibrahim told me, he could not get this miracle out of his mind. One night, a few weeks after Arif had returned to his normal healthy self, God spoke His amazing peace into Ibrahim's heart. He knew at that instant that Ruth's God was the true God. He chose then and there to make her God *his* God.[4]

In the morning, he woke his wife up with this news. Can you imagine her excitement? Later that day he phoned Ruth's pastor asking him to visit them. The pastor must have sensed the urgency in his spirit because he changed his plans and came over right away.

Quietly, yet boldly, Ibrahim confessed his faith in Jesus. Three months later he was baptized, and he has never looked back. Despite various pressures from his family, he has remained steadfast. Praise be to God!

Isn't this a thrilling story of God's grace? God is still in the work of changing people's hearts. You can look to Him to change Layla's heart, too. And, just as He kept Ruth's faith vibrant during her years of waiting for God to open Ibrahim's heart, He can keep the fire of your son Silas' faith alight.

So don't let doubts dull your fervour in praying for God's power to work in Silas' and Layla's lives.[5] Keep praying, and keep loving them. You may be heavy with grief, but there will come a day when your hearts will overflow with joy as you witness the fruit of God's faithfulness in their changed lives.

May the fragrance of your lives richly bless the lives of your Silas and Layla.[6]

Your brother in Christ,

Graham

Notes:

[1] Psalm 55:22; Matthew 11:28-30; 1 Peter 5:7

[2] Romans 15:6; Ephesians 1:3; 1 Peter 1:3

[3] Matthew 5:16

[4] Ruth 1:15, 16

[5] Romans 4:20, 21

[6] 1 Corinthians 13:13; 2 Corinthians 2:14

NINE

A TOUGH DECISION

To: Phoebe_David@OnTheWay.net
From: Graham@KingJesus.net.au
Subject: Your promotion

Hi Phoebe and David,

I was excited to receive your email a few days ago. I value our friendship and so I'm very glad that via emails and SMS messages we can stay in close contact with each other.

How I rejoiced to read how God continues to keep His hand upon your children. It's hard to believe that soon Judith will be a teenager, and then in a couple of years' time Thomas will join her in this once-in-a-lifetime teen adventure!

I heartily congratulate you, David, for the recent offer of promotion from the director of the Telecommunications

Department. This is yet another recognition of your competence as a communications guru and also of your outstanding leadership qualities. Phoebe, you must be very proud of your husband's achievements—and rightfully so.

Do you remember all the sweat and tears of those five years of study here on campus? I recall a few times when you were unable to attend our student Bible studies because of yet another major exam or assignment due the next day. Yet in the end your hard labour produced good results.

But as you said in your email, the promotion also raises some hard questions. For example, how would the move impact your children's future? I'm encouraged that you are asking such questions as they demonstrate your willingness to respond to major life issues as a believer, rather than just assuming that the will and wishes of your director are also God's will.

As I have pondered the issues you raised, I've thought of a few positive reasons for accepting this promotion, and also one or two negative ones. No doubt you have already reflected long and hard on both sides of this decision.

First, the *positive* factors of the offer. One obvious advantage would be the significant increase in your salary. Of course, material gains don't always result in spiritual gains.[1] However, continuing to look on the positive side, you could increase your giving to help people with special needs. And certainly the higher income would help with the rising costs of educating your children.

A more senior position would also enhance your prospects for climbing even higher in the Telecommunications

Department. David, what an exciting challenge for you to test your leadership abilities! I pray that God will guide your footsteps according to His plan for your lives.[2]

I'd also like to highlight a less obvious positive factor—the potential for you to influence many people in the Department through the witness of your life as a true Christian, considering the probability that you would be the only Christian among your fellow-workers. Through your life, your colleagues and friends would be given a unique opportunity to see and hear God's Good News.

So it is possible that God is the One who has orchestrated this promotion. Could it be that it is His plan to send you there first and foremost as His ambassadors,[3] not for the material benefits? If this is the case, then He will also empower and equip you to be strong and steadfast in your faith, no matter what tactics the devil might employ in order to weaken your love for Jesus.

However, if your primary reason for accepting this promotion would be for material and human gain—though I'm sure it would not—I would be concerned lest the enemy use the difficult spiritual environment to weaken or undermine your faith in Jesus.

With all my heart, dear David and Phoebe, I urge you not to make the move unless you are fully convinced that it is *God* who has planned it and is sending you there as His servants.

If you believe so, keep testing God's leading. Let God check and double-check the thoughts and motives of your hearts.[4] I emphasize this because one of Satan's most successful approaches is to gain access to our hearts via our self-centred, self-focused desires.[5]

Now for a *negative* factor or two. For me, one of the most obvious negatives is separation from your church family and the spiritual nurture you receive there. Your whole family presently benefits by attending worship services and fellowship activities, and from contact with Christians in your community and office.

In contrast, in your new location there are just one or two small congregations; the majority follow other religious paths. Perhaps the two of you, as mature believers, would learn to cope with the relative spiritual isolation after moving from a large and lively city church.

My greater concern is for Judith and Thomas and the adjustments they would need to make in such an alien spiritual environment. From the large group of Christian friends they have in your church they would now have just one or two other Christians of their age.

What makes this issue even more difficult is that within the next few years, both Thomas and Judith will be crossing over into adolescence—with all the added stresses and struggles of being teenagers.

We all know from personal experience that our teen years bring on a crisis of identity—who am I? In our earlier years, we found the answer to this question in our relationships at home with our parents and family.

But as we enter puberty, our relationships with our peers begin to play a decisive role in determining how we think and feel about ourselves. We could be thrown in among some tough non-Christian schoolmates, but having a strong, supportive group of Christian friends around us, helps us to stay on track spiritually.

Did either of you experience this in your teen years? I did. During the week at school, I would sometimes be ridiculed for my Christian convictions. But on weekends I experienced acceptance from my friends in our church youth group. Spending time with them each Sunday significantly helped me to accept the differences between myself as a believer and other teenagers.

No matter where Judith and Thomas go to school, they will face such tests as followers of Jesus. But let's remember that in just a few short years, they will begin to form boy-girl relationships from among their circle of friends. If at that time there are hardly any other Christians at school or in the neighbourhood, they could fall in love with a non-Christian—which could even lead to marriage.

I am not forgetting the invaluable role that you as parents are playing in their physical, emotional and spiritual development. I know how faithful you are in reading the Bible and praying daily with your children, and I'm sure you will maintain this family tradition no matter where you live. You've been instilling God's truth in Thomas' and Judith's minds since their infancy, and this will certainly leave its imprint upon them.[6]

Nonetheless, as they enter this new phase in their development, your influence over their choices—including their choice of 'special friends'—will gradually decline. You can still offer them advice or issue the occasional warning. But the opinions and ideas of their peers will become increasingly influential. This may have long term consequences.

Dear David and Phoebe, I truly empathize with you in your struggle. I know how hard it is to weigh up the positives and the negatives, and discern God's mind, in the process of making decisions with far-reaching implications. For this reason I'm often praying for you, asking God to make you wise and show you *His* way ahead in regard to this promotion.

If God leads you to say 'yes' to this promotion, then trust Him to give you the right solutions for the weighty issues I've just mentioned. One possible answer could be to leave your children with a caring Christian family, possibly one of your relatives or a family from your church. Judith and Thomas could then come to stay with you during their long school vacations.

I know that you would all find the separation heart-wrenching, especially at first. But if God leads you to accept the promotion and to leave your children with another family, He will also give divine strength to endure the pain of separation.

But if God leads you to say 'no', you will still need to lean on Him for help. Your director may not agree with your decision. He could treat it as a sign of disloyalty to the Department and you could find your job under threat as a result. But if your true Director is Jesus, He will stand alongside you, giving you the inner strength to cope with all obstacles, and providing you a way to overcome them.[7]

No matter how He leads you, rest at peace in God's perfect knowledge of all your present and future needs as a family. He has promised to show you the way you should go.[8]

Dear Phoebe and David, we may be far from you in body, but in spirit we feel very close. God's Spirit, who lives within you and me, is even closer. He is your true Source of divine knowledge, wisdom and truth.[9] With God's great love, I'm confident that you will make a wise and good decision.

Your fellow-pilgrim and brother in Christ,

Graham

Notes:

[1] Matthew 6:24; 2 Timothy 4:10
[2] Psalms 25:4; 31:3; 48:14; 73:23-24
[3] 2 Corinthians 5:20
[4] Psalm 139:23, 24
[5] Proverbs 14:12; Jeremiah 17:9,10
[6] 2 Timothy 3:14, 15; Ephesians 6:4; Proverbs 22:6
[7] 1 Corinthians 10:13
[8] Isaiah 30:21; Proverbs 3:5, 6
[9] Isaiah 11:1-5; Ephesians 1:17

Ten

Not Alone in the Search

Dear Andrew and Esther,

What a delight to hear your voices over the phone the other day! It brought back wonderful memories of the two nights we stayed with you last year on our way to the mountains.

Thank you, dear friends, for your kind invitation for me to share in your journey of helping Damaris find a believing husband. Truly the choice of a partner for our children is one of life's most crucial decisions.

I sense that you are anxious about Damaris' friendships with young people of other faiths. Perhaps you sometimes wish she wasn't so friendly and gregarious!

Your concerns about her relationships are normal parental feelings. However, you can also be thankful that she is able to relate well with Christians and non-Christians.[1] Remember that, as a true believer, Damaris has a loving Shepherd who guides and guards her wherever she may be.

But as Christian parents, how should you choose a life partner for her? (May I also add *together with her*? I understand that in your culture the parents play a leading role in selecting a husband. Yet Damaris is not only your daughter, she is also your 'sister' in the Lord. You should therefore see her as a spiritually and emotionally mature adult.)

As I was pondering your request I thought of Abraham and Sarah and the exciting story about how God helped them find a believing wife for Isaac, their son of promise. (If you can, read the story now in Genesis 24.)

Let me share three vital lessons from Abraham's life. The *first lesson* is Abraham's determination to find a wife for Isaac who was also a worshipper of the true and living God.

Abraham formerly worshipped idols, like everyone else in his home city of Ur in Babylonia, but now he worshipped God and lived in Canaan. Although Canaanite beliefs and life-styles were similar to the rituals and sacrifices of Ur, he had left all of that behind—forever.

So Abraham wouldn't dream of finding Isaac a wife from among the idol-worshipping Canaanites.[2] He knew that their daughters would bring with them religious beliefs, practices and ways of living which were utterly opposed to God's truth and God's ways.

He decided to send his servant to find a wife from among those in his extended family who had also moved away from Ur and its idolatry. In doing so, Abraham was not motivated by racial, ethnic or family pride. Rather he was acting decisively and responsibly as a man of conviction.

No doubt Abraham could have found a beautiful and cultured young woman for Isaac in a neighbouring Canaanite family. You may also meet well-mannered young men among Damaris' non-Christian friends. You might think, 'This one could make a fine son-in-law'.

But despite their positive qualities, friends like this are foreigners to God's grace. They don't know the ways of our God. They follow a path very different to our Christian walk and ways.[3]

Abraham's example teaches us to focus on the hidden things of the heart rather than on the shallow and transient externals of physical beauty or social position. What you most desire for Damaris is a man with inner beliefs and values that are firmly grounded upon the rock of God's truth. Such a man will establish with her a home of strength, stability and steadfastness of faith and purpose.

Values and beliefs are so important in marriage. Take integrity and honesty. Sadly, not all Christians tell the truth. But as followers of Jesus the Truth,[4] we are indeed called to speak and live the truth.[5]

Are other people required to live by this standard? Whether religious or not, many seem instead to be governed by expediency—whatever will give them the greatest personal gain. Certainly for Damaris you wouldn't want a marriage filled with distrust and suspicion.

Another example is divorce. You know that the Bible's teaching on marriage and divorce is far different than the practice of other religions. At the heart of our Christian view is God's command to remain faithful to our partner until death.[6]

Dear Andrew and Esther, I am confident that you will give Damaris' hand only to a man who is a true follower of Jesus—a man whose character is shaped by God's truth.

A *second lesson* from Abraham's life is his awareness of a unique, God-given calling upon him and his descendants. God had appeared to Abraham and summoned him to trust Him and obey His commands.[7] Through him, God would establish a new nation—a people whom He would call *'My treasured possession.'*[8]

The more Abraham came to know this God, the God above all gods, the more he understood, with the eye of faith, what lay ahead for his descendants—a life of blessing far greater than he would experience in his own lifetime.

God placed in Abraham's soul a sense of destiny and helped him to grasp some of the far-reaching implications of His promises. That included who would make a suitable wife for Isaac. The promised blessings for Abraham's descendants could only be fulfilled if Isaac continued along the same path of faith in the one, eternal God.

This implied that Isaac would also need a wife who would partner with him in carrying out God's plan. Through such a marriage the promised blessings would continue to flow into the following generations.

The same principle applies to all Abraham's descendants—including you and me, who are descendants by faith.[9] God gives each of us the responsibility to keep living as His faithful ones, and to train our children to follow the same path.[10]

Dear Esther and Andrew, as I've already said, Damaris is more to you than just a daughter by descent. She is also one of God's chosen servants through whom He wants to channel His blessings to succeeding generations. Yet this can only happen if Damaris' husband is a fellow-heir, by faith, of these blessings.

Let's go one step further and catch God's vision for Damaris. Her marriage can be one of His ways to spread the fragrant knowledge of Jesus through her family and out into the community and world. What a high calling—to bless people, nations and generations for the glory of God!

A *third and final lesson* from Abraham's life is about his faith and faithfulness. Abraham is widely known for his steadfast faith in God. But he also lapsed into fear and unbelief. When he lied to Pharaoh, saying that Sarah was his sister,[11] Abraham gave in to his fear of man[12] (although he had good reason to fear the despotic Pharaoh).

Yet even Abraham's failures could not stop God from carrying out His promise to bless him and his household for all generations.

So in your search, don't let occasional battles with fear and anxiety dim your vision of God's unshakeable faithfulness. Reread Genesis 24 and be sure of God's power and love. He will guide you to the right person, at the right time and in the right place.

The way He will guide you will be different than the way He guided Abraham and his servant in finding a wife for Isaac—but it will be just as miraculous! Furthermore, the gift for Damaris will be just as special as Rebekah, the beautiful gift He gave to Isaac.

How can I make such a bold statement? Because Abraham's God is also your God. He's none other than the infinite God who rules over the entire universe—including the smallest parts of His creation, even your lives and ours.

Dear Esther and Andrew, trust wholly in Him. You are not alone in this search. God is with you from start to finish. He is the *Author and Finisher* of your faith.[13]

I encourage you to discuss what I've shared. Talk openly and honestly about your feelings and your concerns. Help one another to put on faith as your shield and breastplate.[14] Pray together and commit this most important matter into God's faithful care. He will not fail you!

We will keep praying with you until you receive the fruit of your faith—the believing man who will one day become Damaris' life partner.

Your brother in God's family of the faithful,

Graham

Notes:

[1] Matthew 5:16; Colossians 4:5
[2] Genesis 24:1-3
[3] Ephesians 2:11,12; John 8:12
[4] John 1:14,17; 14:6
[5] Ephesians 4:15,25; 1 John 1:5-7

[6] Matthew 19:3-6
[7] Genesis 12:1; Acts 7:1-4
[8] Exodus 19:5; Deuteronomy 7:6; 14:2; Psalm 135:4
[9] Galatians 3:7, 9
[10] Deuteronomy 6:4-9; Proverbs 22:6; Ephesians 6:4
[11] Genesis 12:11-15
[12] Proverbs 29:25
[13] Hebrews 12:2
[14] Ephesians 6:16; 1 Thessalonians 5:8

ELEVEN
ANOTHER MIRACLE

To: Daniel_Susanna@goforit.net
From: Graham@KingJesus.net.au
Subject: Rejoicing with you both!

Dear Daniel & Susanna,
Thank you for your welcome email received this morning. We were very glad to hear that both you and your two beautiful daughters, Salome and Bethany, remain in good health.

Even though it's been a few years since you moved away, we still miss you. You were such wonderful neighbours—like family to us. We will always be thankful for how you helped us through those early days of adjusting to life in this huge city, to say nothing of the difficult adjustments of entering the academic scene on a completely new university campus.

Daniel, we are delighted to see your growing reputation as a genetics scholar. You are a wonderful example to other Christian scientists, proving that it is possible to be both a scientist and a true follower of Jesus.

We commend you, too, Susanna, for serving so wholeheartedly alongside your beloved husband. You have proven yourself to be a true companion to Daniel and a dedicated mother to Salome and Bethany. How blessed they are to have such faithful, caring parents.

We were interested to read about Salome's break-up with Ali. Some months ago a mutual friend told us about their relationship. But now we praise God with you for His answer to your prayers. At the same time we continue to pray for Salome, who, as you wrote, is feeling lonely and lost.

I was touched by your decision *not* to pressure Salome to make the break with Ali. You knew that she was moving into spiritually dangerous territory.[1] But you also understood, with her temperament and personality, that using heavy-handed tactics to force her to end the relationship would have created a serious rift between parents and daughter.

I also think you did the right thing in supporting Salome in her marriage plans rather than adopting a 'who cares?' attitude. What a wonderful example of unconditional love! This kept Salome's heart open to you, and also to God.

Now what? You have a very needy daughter at home. You are aware of and still concerned about Ali's needs, too, since he was an integral part of your family circle for over a year. And you can't deny having needs of your own.

It's these different needs that are on my heart as I write. First, how can you help meet Salome's needs? Though she has made a wise decision, it will take time before her heart catches up with her head. Certainly we cannot blame her for having topsy-turvy emotions, as if she were unstable. Who made us with emotions? Didn't Jesus Himself also experience anger, sorrow and joy?[2]

So don't be overly concerned if Salome expresses deep disappointment or even anger. Don't take such outbursts personally, as if they are directed against you for something you have said or done. Refuse to allow emotional words to penetrate the defences of your hearts.

What she needs right now is not a lot of words, but a lot of affection and understanding, and a lot of prayer. I know that this is what you want to give her, even though you feel weak within yourselves.

Second, a few words of advice about your relationship with Ali. It is a wonderful testimony of God's grace that you can write about your love for him and your anxiety that, in despair, he might harm himself.

Although you may like Ali as a person, you must draw new boundaries in your relationship with him. You can still be friendly and cordial when you meet him around town, but it would be unwise to retain a close friendship link with him. That would be unkind for Salome, don't you agree?

Focus your prayers and thoughts on his deepest need for a living relationship with Jesus. Pray that God will stir up a passionate longing within him to reach beyond any religious rituals to the very heart of God. Salome made her decision because she wanted to obey her Lord's will. May this convince him that there is something of infinite value in her Christian faith.

Have you considered expressing your esteem for him in a brief note? You could show your appreciation for the positive character traits you have seen in him—his respectful attitude to you, for example, or his kind and thoughtful ways with Salome.

Assure him that your differences in religious beliefs do not make him in your eyes any less a person of worth and significance. In saying this, you will be expressing one of the core truths about God, that He has no favourites.[3]

Beloved Daniel and Susanna, if you are able to write such a letter, you can be sure that it will make a strong impression on Ali. How often would he receive a letter of love and concern in similar circumstances? Perhaps he's thinking that as Salome's parents you want nothing more to do with him. Why not surprise him?

Third, a few thoughts just for you. By God's grace, you've both come through the pains and heartache of the past fourteen months. He has helped you to keep supporting one another, and kept you from allowing your personal pain to erupt as angry outbursts towards one another. This unity as husband and wife, father and mother, has had a far greater impact upon Salome than you might realize.

However, the battle isn't over yet. The enemy knows the strength of your unity and will use every possible tactic and trick in order to break through your defences. So stay on sentry duty. Work hard, especially on those days when one of you is emotionally low and vulnerable. More than ever, that's when you need kind words rather than angry reactions.

Expect that at times you will feel positive and hopeful about God's plan for Salome and her future marriage partner. But don't be dismayed or aghast if you struggle. At other times you may doubt that God will meet Salome's needs and work everything out for her good.[4]

Remember to encourage one another daily with words that help you to keep trusting God for Salome's future.[5]

If you would like to share this email with Salome and Bethany, of course you have our agreement. Please pass on our love to them, assuring them that we continue to pray for them both. And we won't stop praying that in His perfect timing, God will lead the life's partner of *His* choosing into each of their lives. May He give them both the grace and the patience to wait until then.

I'd better close so I can collect my papers and books for my next lecture, which begins in just half an hour.

Looking forward to another email from you soon,

Your brother in Christ,

Graham

Notes:

[1] 1 Kings 11:1-4; 16:30-32

[2] Mark 3:5; Luke 10:21; John 11:35

[3] Acts 10:34, 35

[4] Mark 9:24

[5] Hebrews 3:12, 13

TWELVE

'I'M TO BLAME!'

Dear Lydia,

Thank you for your good letter. Yes, of course I remember meeting you at your annual church conference two years ago. I remember how Michael, like a typical teenager, was embarrassed to be around his mother.

What I most remember was how you cried as you told me of your beloved husband's sudden death when Michael was just a baby. The pain of such a loss stays with us for so long, doesn't it?

And now you are battling yet another sadness.

Yes, I will try to contact Michael. He isn't one of my students, but I will find a good reason to invite him over for a chat. Perhaps if I mention the word 'food', he won't be able to refuse! (Please don't worry—I won't tell him that you wrote to me.)

Your news that Michael intends to move in with a group

of non-Christian friends—including young women—is distressing. I share your concerns for his moral and spiritual welfare. Sadly, living in mixed households has become a widely accepted lifestyle among university students. Some of them say that it is cheaper that way, but I think it sometimes has more to do with enjoying their 'freedoms'.

But Michael will be vulnerable to the corrupting influences of that 'freedom' if he goes ahead with his plan.[1] He will discover that living among people whose beliefs and morals are opposed to God's truth can easily drag him into the same current of behaviour.

You have every right to feel concerned for your precious son. I promise to make time for a good discussion with him.

But I'm also concerned for *you*, dear sister in Christ. From your letter it's clear that your heart is burdened with anxiety. How hard to imagine that your only child—whom you faithfully sent to Sunday school and a Christian school—could be so quickly pulled into this circle of non-Christian friends.

Dear Lydia, there are probably two reasons why Michael is being tempted in this way. First, he's just left the security of his home and closeknit circle of friends in your small town. For the first time in his life, he's experiencing the fascination and 'fun' of big city freedoms.

Second, his new situation away from home is confronting him with a crisis of faith. You've given him a loving, secure home, and I have every reason to believe you have been a faithful mother. But when Christian young people encounter the myriad temptations of university life, inevitably their faith is tested.

I'm also wondering if Michael's faith up to now has been the Christianity of his parents. If so, we must pray that he experiences a living, *personal* faith in Jesus Christ. Let's ask God to use this testing so that he will begin building his life upon Jesus Christ, the only sure foundation for a living faith.[2]

I will also pray that God will help you leave all your anxiety over Michael with Him, because He cares for you.[3]

But what's all this about your failures as a mother—as if almost twenty years of hard work, love and sacrifice is evaporating into thin air? 'If only I had been a better mother! If only I had been more diligent in teaching him the Bible!'

In moments of discouragement, it's easy to become lost in regret. Lydia, every parent fails to live up to her (or his) own expectations, as well as the expectations of her children. That's when the evil one whispers, 'You are an absolute failure!'

But what a lie! You have been a faithful and devoted mother to Michael. Even though it's been so hard for you to juggle home responsibilities with full-time work, still you have been God's servant in your little family circle. Lydia, you are *not* to blame for anything that is happening in Michael's life!

You must also guard lest Satan attack your peace of mind with another lie: 'God is to blame for your husband's death, and for leaving Michael to grow up in a fatherless home.' Have you ever thought that if only Michael had grown up with a father, he would now be a strong Christian?

Dear sister, has God failed you since your husband's homecall? Has He left you alone? Hasn't He rather always been there, an Unseen Presence in your home as you raised Michael?

Has He not led you through the deep waters of loneliness and heartache?[4] Truly, He has never failed to keep His promises to you.[5]

So will God fail you now? Will He be unfaithful to you and to Michael in this crisis? His constant faithfulness is the very thing about which you can be absolutely *certain*, now and always.[6]

So banish your fears. Stem the flow of all those 'if onlys' in your mind. Instead commit your way and the ways of Michael into God's strong and loving hands.[7] Trust Him to work a miracle in Michael's mind and life.

How and when God accomplishes His work in Michael is up to Him. Please don't lose confidence in His promises, as God may first let Michael go through a time of hurt and heart-searching. Even if Michael goes ahead with his plan, this does not mean God has not heard your prayers. If Michael is strongwilled, he won't surrender to God without a fight—and some wounding in the process.

Dear Lydia, you can be sure that God will deal lovingly with your son—gently, but also firmly. God's gentle Spirit will remind him of His truth, which you and others have instilled in him.[8]

But God will also show Michael a tough love, especially if he refuses to heed our warnings and pleas and counsel. With perfect wisdom, He will turn up the heat in Michael's life until he gives up the fight and surrenders to Infinite Love.

Isn't that what happened in Jesus' parable of the prodigal son?[9] While the son was away in the far country with everything going his way—money, friends, pleasure—his father and home were furthest from his mind. When did he decide to return home? When all these false props were blown away and he reached the pits—the stench and filth of the pigsty, starving in body and broken within. Only then was he ready to re-enter the real world—the world of his father and 'home'.

Jesus' message through this parable is the Good News that *God loves sinners* and longs for them to return home.[10] And this includes your beloved Michael. Believe me, you have God on your side as you pray for Michael to come to his senses and return to his heavenly Father.

What can you do as you wait? Above all, pray for him. Let me suggest two prayers. First, ask God to break Satan's hold over Michael's mind and desires, stirring within him a desperate longing to enjoy the *true* freedom that only Jesus can give.[11]

Second, ask God to guide you as you express, in word and action, your love for Michael.

Focus your prayers upon his coming to his spiritual senses, praying that God's Spirit will reveal how lost he will be without Jesus at the centre of his life.

Dear sister in Christ, there is nothing that you can do for Michael with greater potential to change the direction of his life than to pray for him.[12] Take comfort and be encouraged, because God delights in answering the prayers of His people,[13] for the glory of His name.

I hope I will be able to write again with encouraging news after my time with Michael. You are in my thoughts and prayers.

Your brother and friend,

Graham

Notes:

[1] 1 Corinthians 15:33

[2] 1 Corinthians 3:11

[3] 1 Peter 5:7

[4] Isaiah 43:1-3

[5] Hebrews 13:5

[6] Lamentations 3:19-26

[7] Psalms 37:3-7; 62:11,12

[8] Psalm 78:5-7

[9] Luke 15:11-32

[10] Luke 19:10

[11] John 8:32,36

[12] Matthew 7:7-11; James 5:16b; 1 John 3:21,22; 5:14,15

[13] Proverbs 15:8

Section Three

Letters to Marrieds

THIRTEEN
WORTH THE WAIT

Dear John and Shyla,

I've been so excited since receiving your letter last week with the wonderful news of Shyla's baptism.

If only we could have been there, dear Shyla. I can imagine that John was fighting back tears of joy as he witnessed the fruit of his prayers—the divine miracle of your joining him as a fellow-heir of God's grace.[1]

The nine-year prayer journey to that day, John, must at times have felt like an eternity! We've been asking our great God to help you persevere, in hope and faith, until you received the answer to your prayers.

How we praise God too for His faithfulness in keeping you from compromising your faith. By patiently waiting, you paved the way for Shyla to taste the freedom we experience when we trust in Jesus. Your patience has been rewarded.

John, I have a special request. In recent years God has been bringing me into contact with believers who are married to non-Christians.

I think other believers can learn important lessons from the witness of your life over these past nine years. Would you mind if I shared some of your story with them? My goal is to offer guidelines to God's people on how to relate effectively with their non-Christian spouse, for the glory of God.

John, there are five strengths I have seen in you through your marriage. I have observed God's work of grace in your life, and that your testimony has great potential for encouraging other believers.

So let's begin with *the first strength—your patience in waiting for God's timing.* Instead of trying to push Shyla into God's kingdom, with wisdom and patience you allowed her to hold on to her own beliefs.[2] You were waiting for God to prepare the way—to bring her to a realization that her inherited beliefs were not bringing peace and contentment.

I recall a long talk we had soon after we met at an annual believers' retreat. You were there alone and were seriously missing Shyla. Do you remember? You were still newlyweds. I encouraged you to take every oppoprtunity to share your faith with Shyla. I'll never forget your answer: 'True love cannot be forced to grow and develop into a healthy plant.' Thank you for balancing my zeal with your wisdom.

Of course you hoped that Shyla would one day choose Jesus as her Saviour and Master. However, God gave you the discernment to see that if she was to make a genuine commitment, it must begin with *God's Spirit* working in her mind and heart, not with persistent persuasion.

I praise God that He gave you this understanding because this is what prepared her for the difficulties she would later face with her family.

The second strength I've noted is your respect for Shyla. You probably remember writing to me several years ago about how spiritual oneness was the missing link in your marriage. Shyla was then showing little outward interest in spiritual things. Her priority was her business career and all the nice 'extras' that money can buy. She was often indifferent even about her own religious duties.

Yet even when you shared this, you spoke positively and respectfully about Shyla's diligence as a wife, mother and business woman. So many husbands criticize or bad-mouth their wives around their friends, often revealing personal or family secrets. What a positive contrast!

I truly respect you, John, for your attitude towards Shyla. You were probably unaware of what was happening during this time, but God was slowly working in Shyla's heart through your life as she began to 'see' the Good News of Jesus.

In all marriages, even mature Christians can say things to their loved ones that they later regret, especially in times of stress, tension or disappointment. Perhaps there have been such times, behind closed doors, for you. Yet I am confident that God has been shining the light of His Gospel through your life in the home through your respect for her.

The third strength is the honour you have shown your own

parents and also Shyla's parents. Again I have seen this mainly through your conversation. But I believe the same spirit is evident when you are face-to-face with either set of parents.

Perhaps it has been more difficult to show godly attitudes towards Shyla's parents. It must not have been easy to respond respectfully when they spoke derogatively about your Christian faith and traditions.

Whenever we come under attack because of our faith, our natural tendency is to fight back with words, or to think of ways of getting even. But this only makes matters worse and raises tensions. How blessed when we choose to be peacemakers.[3] You have sowed seeds of unity and peace that have triumphed over the weeds of discord.

I commend you for honouring Shyla's parents and your own parents. In doing so, you honour God through your obedience to His command: *'Honor your father and your mother; so that you may live long in the land the LORD your God is giving you.'*[4]

And, as you wrote, you have reaped the fruit—honour from your beloved wife and a good relationship with her parents. Praise God, John. Could this have been one of the keys to Shyla's heart, in answer to your prayers?[5] Would you agree with this comment, dear Shyla?

The fourth strength is your trust in God. Do you recall when you once wrote to me, 'One day she *will* believe'? You may not have realized it at the time but your sincere trust in God's faithfulness also encouraged me to keep praying in faith for Shyla's salvation.

Finally, *the fifth strength—your faithfulness in the life of your church*. I believe your faithfulness has reaped spiritual benefits in your own life, and in the lives of your wife and children. For yourself, you have the blessings of encouragement from fellow-believers; for your children, the blessings of your training from God's Word; and for Shyla, the blessings of Christian friends who visit and join your home fellowships.

Of course this exposure can have its down-side too. We Christians can be stumbling blocks in the path of non-believers, inhibiting them from hearing God's most wonderful message. I wonder if Shyla ever saw prejudice or heard critical comments against her own religion.

The miracle of Shyla's believing in Jesus affirms the central truth that salvation is from God, not man.[6] As the church of Jesus Christ, we always fall short of God's perfect standards—and the expectations of other people.

Yet even though Shyla may have been troubled (as we are too) by the unhelpful witness of some Christians, she has lived with your consistent example. As a result, her heart has slowly but surely become open to God's true gospel message in Jesus.

John, my dear brother, what do you think? May I use your story as an example? Consider its potential to bless, encourage and instruct God's people who are facing the same struggles.

I look forward to hearing from you soon. Dear Shyla, Frieda sends warm and loving greetings to you.

Your brother in Christ,

Graham

P.S.: Please do me a favour and mail us a photo of Shyla's special service and also a recent family photo. Many thanks.

Notes:

[1] 1 Peter 3:7; Acts 18:1-3, 18-19, 26; Romans 16:3
[2] Proverbs 19:11
[3] Matthew 5:9; Hebrews 12:14; James 3:13-18
[4] Exodus 20:12; Deuteronomy 5:16; Ephesians 6:2, 3
[5] 1 Samuel 2:30; 1 John 3:21, 22
[6] Romans 11:36; Ephesians 2:4, 5; Colossians 2:13, 14

FOURTEEN
STAND FAST

Dear Anjali,

I greet you in the precious name of our Lord Jesus.

I am truly thankful to your dear friend, Martha, for agreeing to hand-carry this letter to you. Martha is our friend, too. She is the one who told us about the opposition you have been facing from your husband Kamal.

When Martha told us about your situation, I immediately felt a strong desire to write to you. Although I don't know you personally, Anjali, I have been burdened to pray for you. Other brothers and sisters in our church family are also sharing in your trials through prayer. We've been asking our gracious Father in heaven to give you a firm resolve to remain true to Jesus, regardless of the outcome of your present ordeal.

We were deeply moved, Anjali, when Martha told us how she met you on the train a few months ago—on the very day you were thinking of taking your life! Praise God, who rescued you from such a tragic end.

Martha also told us that before turning to Christ you had no purpose in life. You considered yourself a failure because you had not been able to give your husband a child. Now you have a new life and purpose in Jesus Christ!

But your new-found faith in Jesus Christ is obviously *not* good news to your husband! It must be so hard to deal with his fierce anger and frequent threats of divorce.

I can imagine the kind of questions you're asking. 'How can Kamal react like this? Before I put my trust in Jesus, I was sullen and difficult. Doesn't he see that I've changed, and that our home life and relationship are better for it? . . . Was it just bad luck that I sat beside Martha on the train? . . . What if Kamal does divorce me? Where will I live? Who will take care of me?'

Dear sister in the Lord, this is a very painful time for you. Your thoughts are consumed by Kamal's threats and what might happen to you. But God wants you to see that behind Kamal's intimidating behaviour lie dark spiritual forces that are bent on extinguishing God's light within you.[1]

The real battle is not with Kamal but with our enemy, Satan, and his evil forces. Since Satan can't vent his anger on Jesus, he turns on His followers, threatening and intimidating them in the hope that they will turn back to their old ways.[2]

So guard against the thought that *you* are the cause of Kamal's anger and hatred. Nothing could be further from the truth.

What you need to remember is that you are not alone in this battle. Jesus spoke powerful words of encouragement to

His first disciples: *'And surely I am with you always, to the very end of the age.'*[3] These words are recorded in the Bible because they are for us, too. So whenever Kamal lashes out with angry threats or physical force, repeat Jesus' promise silently to yourself ('I am with *you*, Anjali, my dear child'), knowing that He will always be faithful to you.

The Bible uses another powerful picture to describe our peace in Him. The devil attacks us with fiery darts, aiming to weaken our faith in Jesus. But we can respond by holding up *the shield of faith*—that is, by actively putting our trust in Jesus, our Defender and Shield.[4]

When Kamal goes on the attack, reaffirm in your heart your trust in Jesus. Remember His victory over all Satan's powers *on your behalf.*[5] He fought and triumphed over Satan through His cross so that everyone who clings to His cross for protection might also triumph over Satan's attacks against them.

And there's more. Jesus not only won that all-decisive contest with Satan 2,000 years ago for you, He *continues* to fight for you. He stands in your defence against Satan's accusations, interceding before the Father's throne for you.[6]

How awesome that we have this great Conqueror fighting on our side! It's true, Anjali, no matter how often your mind or your feelings tell you otherwise. You cannot see Him (yet), but with the eye of faith you can see Him pleading for you in the presence of His Father and yours.

So ask God to keep your feet firm and steady on Jesus, the Rock, unmoved by any fierce winds that Satan stirs up against you. Whenever Kamal's hot words fly like fiery darts, remind yourself, 'Jesus is my Rock; I will not be moved'. God will honour this trust and give you His peace in the midst of the storm.[7]

Something else I want to share with you is that no one can live through such stress as you're presently facing and not feel troubled. I'm sure you feel upset and hurt when you face Kamal's anger. Your natural inclination would be to retaliate.

Guard against the desire to hurt him for hurting you. Rather follow Jesus' example. When His enemies and accusers mocked Him, He refused to retaliate. Instead, He spoke words of blessing and forgiveness: *'Father, forgive them, for they do not know what they are doing.'*[8]

Anjali, repeat this prayer for Kamal's sake. Pray for him, even while he is venting his anger and threats on you. Ask the Father to set him free from the passions that keep him enslaved to the evil one.

Other prayers that Jesus uttered from His cross may also become yours in your moments of deepest distress. Have you ever felt as if God has deserted you? Remember Jesus' cry of anguish, *'My God, my God, why have you forsaken me?'*[9]

Be encouraged, knowing that God will never forsake you. Rather He will walk with you through each dark valley.[10]

At the end of Jesus' suffering He prayed, *'Father, into your hands I commit my spirit.'*[11] God invites you, Anjali, to commit your spirit into His safe and secure hands. Just as God heard the prayer of His beloved Son on the cross and strengthened Him to endure, He will hear your prayer as you commit your life into His strong and loving hands.

How will He answer? Maybe He will rescue you from the trial. Or He may add grace so that you will have the inner strength to endure more trials.[12] *How* He answers is His prerogative; *that* He answers is our certainty!

He could even do a mirracle in Kamal's heart, giving him the irresistible desire to bow his knee before Jesus, confessing Him: *'My Lord and my God.'* [13]

'Impossible', you may say. But God has been doing miracles of salvation for centuries—and He hasn't changed! He has the power and the will to save Kamal.[14]

No matter what the outcome may be, one thing is sure—you may expect to taste the goodness and kindness of God.[15]

My dear sister Anjali, may these simple encouragements help you to hold fast in your present struggles. And you will, because your Lord Jesus is with you—your *Rock*, your *Fortress* and your *Deliverer.*[16]

Your brother and fellow-soldier in God's fight,

Graham

P.S.: Please consider destroying this letter if you think that Kamal might find it and use it against you.

Notes:

[1] Ephesians 6:10-12
[2] Revelation 12:17; Nehemiah 4:1-9
[3] Matthew 28:20
[4] Ephesians 6:16; Psalms 7:10; 18:30
[5] Hebrews 2:14, 15
[6] 1 John 2:1, 2; John 17:9-11; Romans 8:34
[7] Matthew 5:11, 12; 1 Corinthians 10:13; 1 Peter 1:3-7
[8] Luke 23:34; 1 Peter 2:21-23; 1 John 2:6
[9] Matthew 27:46
[10] Hebrews 4:14-16
[11] Luke 23:46
[12] 2 Corinthians 12:9
[13] Matthew 27:54; John 20:28
[14] 2 Peter 3:9
[15] Psalm 34:8-10
[16] Psalms 18:2

FIFTEEN
GENUINE LOVE

Dear Joel,

It's been a while since we've been in touch, hasn't it? The last time we were together was the week after your wedding when you and Hanna visited us before setting off for your new posting in the interior. I was excited for you both as I saw your eagerness to face the challenges of your new appointment as a mining engineer.

I was even more excited to talk with you after receiving the announcement of Peter's birth! He would be about six months old by now, wouldn't he?

But now I am forced to get back in contact with you after receiving Hanna's very distressed note. You know how heart-broken she is—and understandably so.

Dear Joel, I'm still asking myself: How could my good friend Joel go away to his head office and engage in an affair?

I simply cannot believe that you, my brother in Christ, would allow this to happen.

Please read on. Don't close your heart to what I want to share with you. I am writing as a friend—someone who is willing to go out on a limb in order to save his friend from disaster, and prepared to speak a hard word *for his friend's good.*[1] You would know that I am speaking in love if you could see my eyes and hear my voice right now.

Joel, you are one of God's beloved children. Yes, God loves you as a son.[2] It was His choice in the first place to save you and adopt you into His eternal family.[3] And He won't stop loving you now even when you do things that displease Him.

But you need to understand your Father's love. It's not like the love of a kindly old grandfather who turns a blind eye to his grandson's mischief.

In contrast, God's love for you is a *genuine* love—a love that will not hide the truth for your good, a love that is willing to wound you if necessary to rescue you from peril.[4]

Out of love, God's love, I cannot remain silent as I hear about this secret liaison. My love for you compels me to call you to renounce your sin. Please, for your own sake and also for the sake of Hanna and Peter—for God's sake—listen to the wisdom of my rebuke and warnings.[5]

I fear that you might react angrily: 'This relationship has nothing to do with my marriage with Hanna. It's nothing more than an occasional liaison when I am away on business. Men have their needs, you know. Life is hard enough with the stresses of work. Can't I have a little comfort?'

Joel, this is the devil's logic—that you have a need for love that you may satisfy by engaging in sexual encounters with whomever you choose and whenever that passion arises.

That idea of love destroys true love. What's more, it cannot but arouse anger and jealousy in the heart of your loving wife—as you have been experiencing!

Above all, your behaviour arouses God's jealous love towards you.[6] Don't be shocked if you feel the sharp sting of God's chastening rod if you continue walking down this path.

God's commandment is clear: *'Do not commit adultery.'*[7] This commandment is an expression of genuine love. Our loving Father has given it to us because He knows that only in holy marital faithfulness can we truly enjoy the delights of sexual love. Thus when God says 'no' to extramarital affairs, He is saying 'yes' and opening the way to a life of true blessedness. Please take a moment to reflect on this, Joel.

This woman may be attractive, but she is driving a wedge between you and your family. She may be 'religious' but she doesn't submit to God's laws. Joel, the signs are clear: DANGER![8]

My friend, this liaison is more than innocent pleasure with a pretty young woman. Satan wants to cut you off from Jesus. I plead with you: Do not give him any more ground! Listen to God's call through me, and also through Hanna. Be wise and heed our advice and correction.

Remember Solomon? At the beginning of his reign as Israel's king, he asked God for wisdom so that he might lead his people wisely and justly.[9] God answered his prayer by making him the wisest person on earth.

But Solomon did not always *act* wisely. Renowned among the nations for his great wisdom and knowledge, he began to walk according to the wisdom of the world. He forged political alliances with foreign kings by marrying their daughters for political advantage.[10]

This may have been politically shrewd, but it was spiritually disastrous. Just as God had warned, Solomon's heart strayed from wholehearted worship of his God.[11] He allowed his foreign wives to worship their idols and gods within God's holy city, and even joined them in making sacrifices to those gods.

What a tragic ending to such a brilliant beginning—from a flood-tide of God's blessings to the flood-gate of God's judgement upon his family and his kingdom, for generations to come.

There are obvious differences between your story and Solomon's, but the potential for spiritual ruin is the same. God's Spirit is summoning you to take decisive action: to get rid of your wrong ideas about this sinful relationship; to confess your sin honestly and sincerely to Hanna; and to cut all contact with this other woman.

If you follow my counsel, I am confident that Hanna will forgive you. But she will need more reassurance than mere words. You will need to prove that you have chosen to return to a life of marital faithfulness no matter what. It will be your responsibility to rebuild trust by the way you conduct yourself in the everyday affairs of your life, such as faithfully keeping your promises around the home.

Joel, God has not rejected you because you have strayed

momentarily from His pathway. He seeks and longs to bring His wandering sheep back to the fold.[12] Please do not delay in heeding His call.

For obvious reasons, this hasn't been an easy letter to write . . . or an easy one for you to read! Yet it's my earnest prayer and hope that the outcome of my writing to you will be a true and lasting reconciliation with your beloved Hanna. That will also mean returning to the delights of living in an open and loving relationship with your heavenly Father.

Please write me soon with some good news.

Your loving brother in Christ,

Graham

Notes:

[1] Proverbs 17:10; 27:6

[2] John 15:9; Colossians 3:12

[3] John 1:12, 13; Ephesians 1:5

[4] Proverbs 3:11, 12

[5] Proverbs 10:23; 14:16; 15:5

[6] Exodus 20:5; 34:14; Deuteronomy 4:24; 6:14, 15

[7] Exodus 20:14; Deuteronomy 5:18; Matthew 19:18; Romans 13:9; 1 Corinthians 6:9, 10; Hebrews 13:4

[8] Proverbs 6:20-35

[9] 2 Chronicles 1:7-12

[10] 1 Kings 11: 1-3

[11] 1 Kings 11: 4-13; Nehemiah 13: 26

[12] Luke 15:4-7

Sixteen
A Lasting Influence

To: Aisha@computergossip.org
From: Graham@KingJesus.net.au
Subject: Jalil's spiritual development

Hello Aisha!

I received your email yesterday. What a wonderful surprise! You asked if I remember you from my 'Introduction to English Literature' class. To be honest, I had to check back in my records but it didn't take long before I found your name, and also your outstanding marks.

How excited Frieda and I were to read your *most* special news—that you are now a part of our family, God's family. I was especially encouraged to learn that your journey to faith in Jesus began with a spontaneous answer I gave in class one day to a question about Easter.

Then God did the rest, arranging for a Christian lady (you expressed it so beautifully—'a lady with a difference') to move into the apartment next to yours.

Of course you would feel sad and distressed over Hussein's scornful reaction when he found out about your relationship with her. But that's to be expected, don't you think? Although he may not appear serious about his own religious beliefs, he probably feels ashamed before his family, and also before his friends and work colleagues.

But on the positive side, as you wrote, he is a good husband and father to your son, Jalil. Thank God for that! And I'm sure that behind his sometimes abrupt exterior, he's still proud of his lovely wife.

Now to your question: 'What can I do to make sure that Jalil also follows Jesus?' What a superb question. Of course, you hope Hussein will one day come to believe. But for now, it's right that you concentrate on helping young Jalil to understand God's ways and God's great love for him.

Yes, I appreciate your concern that Jalil could learn wrong habits and worldly values from his daddy. However, dear Aisha, you have two distinct advantages: First, you have God and His Word as your Guide for training your son in the ways of truth and righteousness;[1] and second, you have the opportunity to spend many hours every day with Jalil in his formative years.

Now how can you best use these opportunities so that, with God's help, Jalil will want to join you in following our Lord Jesus?

I'd like to answer your good question by telling you the story of two special women. Their names, Eunice and Lois, are mentioned in Paul's second letter to Timothy.[2] Eunice was Timothy's mother and Lois his grandmother. They both were Jewish women who had accepted Jesus as their Messiah.

Eunice, however, was married to an unbelieving Greek. We don't know his name and Paul makes no reference to him or to any influence he might have had on Timothy.[3] Instead he highlights the formative spiritual role that Timothy's mother and grandmother had in his life.[4]

Daily these devoted women taught the Scriptures to Timothy. For them the Old Testament Scriptures were God's Holy Book,[5] given to His chosen people to guide them in the ways of wisdom, and for their eternal blessing.[6] Their faithful training shaped Timothy's thinking, which in turn shaped the way he would later serve God and serve His minister Paul.[7]

Paul first met Timothy when he visited Lystra on one of his missionary journeys. They probably met in the local Jewish synagogue when Timothy was already a disciple of Jesus.[8] From Paul's letters, we learn that Timothy was a young man with an open, sensitive heart for God and for the needs of others. His character qualities and devotion obviously impressed Paul who felt immediately drawn to him.

Paul asked if he could take Timothy along with him. From that point on, Eunice and Lois wouldn't see much of Timothy. No doubt they felt sad as they saw him go. Yet I'm sure that God gave them His peace as they committed Timothy into His care and protection. Can't you imagine their rejoicing whenever they received news how God was using their son and grandson to proclaim and teach His gospel to many people?

Just think of it, dear Aisha—Timothy, once an unknown disciple of Jesus, living a quiet life in his home town, now serving with the great apostle Paul. Isn't it amazing to see how God used Timothy's upbringing to prepare him for his pastoral and evangelistic ministry! And it all began on his mother's knee, without any spiritual support from Timothy's father.

That lack of positive influence from Timothy's father was filled and exceeded by the strong, godly influences of his mother and grandmother. And what a great harvest they reaped when Timothy reached manhood!

Believe me, dear Aisha, God can and will do a similar work through Jalil's life, bringing His light to others when he grows into manhood. The power of God's Word is the same today as it was in Timothy's day.[9]

As you faithfully teach your precious son to know God and obey His commandments and to believe in Jesus, God's Spirit will be imprinting His truth indelibly upon Jalil's young, impressionable mind. At times you may wonder if anything is getting through. Don't be put off by his childish mischief! Trust God to do His work through your faithful training and example. He will accomplish great things in Jalil's heart, mind and life, just as He did in Timothy's.

I want to urge you also to believe God for the impossible: that He will work through Jalil's simple faith and understanding of God to impact his daddy's faith. What an exciting thought for you to store away in your heart—that

Jalil, the apple of his father's eye, could one day become God's messenger and point his daddy to Jesus.

Dear Aisha, I have other things I'd like to share with you but I'll save these for a later email. When you have a chance amid the daily duties of home life and all the demands of caring for a lively young son, please write to us again.

With our love and prayers.

Your brother in Christ,

Graham

P.S.: Please send us a recent photo of you and your little family. It would help me remember you better, and help Frieda and me to pray for you. Many thanks.

Notes:

[1] Proverbs 22:6; Ephesians 6:4
[2] 2 Timothy 1:5
[3] Acts 16:1
[4] 2 Timothy 3:14-15
[5] 2 Timothy 3:16, 17
[6] Psalms 1; 19:7-11
[7] Philippians 2:19-23
[8] Acts 16:1
[9] Hebrews 4:12

SEVENTEEN

DESERTED, BUT NEVER ALONE

My dear Kamila,

I have felt heartsick ever since your parents phoned two days ago with your sad news. Although we all knew that Ahmad might decide to leave you and baby Alesha, we had all hoped for a change of heart.

How terribly painful for you to hear his decision to divorce you. My wife and I both wept, but our tears are nothing compared with yours. But we are comforted to know that the Spirit of our Lord Jesus, who lives in you as one of God's precious people,[1] is comforting and reassuring you of our Father's undying love for you.[2] May He strengthen your heart daily so that you bear up under the weight of your grief.

Your parents told me that you are in turmoil, with feelings of betrayal, anxiety, anger and despair. No wonder! Don't imagine that this is a sign that you are slipping backwards or losing touch with God. Not for one moment! Anyone whose life partner turns his back on their marriage vows cannot but suffer deep emotional pain.

Dear Kamila, God understands what you are feeling. His ear hears the sighs of your broken heart as you look down upon Alesha sleeping. His eyes see the tears on your pillow through those long and lonely nights. The light of His presence is with you no matter how dark the night may seem.

Yes, God sees your heart and identifies with your pain. He knows you wanted to remain faithful to Ahmad, even though you were no longer on the same spiritual path.

I encourage you to acknowledge everything that is happening within you. Instead of trying to convince yourself that things 'should have worked out', accept the ups and downs of your emotions. Try to see them as waves that are breaking, with pounding force, on the shoreline of your heart.

Let me mention some 'waves' that may be striking you these days. First, *waves of sadness and regret*. Have you ever thought, 'If only I hadn't met Ruth in the park? If only I had walked on when she started talking about Jesus! My marriage to Ahmad wasn't perfect, but it was good. Now it's gone. When I told Ahmad of my decision to become a Christian he turned against me. Now he's left us!'

I know that such regrets are just musings of a profoundly sad heart. You know that your decision to follow Jesus has given you a new life, even if it's also brought these trials and heartaches.

God's Word has a lot to teach us about our sufferings as believers. It teaches us that we will reap many blessings if we persevere.[3] This is God's way of encouraging us not to think of our sufferings as harmful, but to expect *blessings* that He gives to those who persevere for Jesus' sake.[4]

For example, remember the unique blessings you have in Christ because God has adopted you into His eternal family. Then offer prayers of thanksgiving and praise, thanking your heavenly Father for all He has so generously given you, as well as for all He has promised you as one of His beloved children. Even if tears fall to earth as your prayers rise to heaven, you can rejoice. To your Father, your tears are a sweet-smelling sacrifice of praise.[5]

Remember also that God has promised to take care of you and Alesha. Ahmad has been your main provider, and in meeting your needs and Alesha's, he's been God's servant. But now that his help is being withdrawn, does this mean that God will withdraw *His* help? Certainly not! Human caregivers may fail us, but God remains faithful. He will provide for all your needs.[6]

You do not need to worry *how* He will do this. All you need to remember is His promise to keep pouring His grace upon you.[7] That's a certainty. *He* is your true Husband and Father, whose faithfulness is as sure as the rising of the sun.

So, dear Kamila, please don't torment yourself with regrets over your step of faith to follow Jesus. Rather rejoice that you now have One who will share all your burdens, because He cares for you.[8] Take heart in His most precious promises.

Second, you are probably also battling *waves of fear and anxiety*. I know from experience that at our lowest moments we become anxious. We worry about how we will cope, but also about such foundational issues as our relationship with God.

You could be thinking that this great sorrow has befallen you because you committed some sin. Now you're suffering God's righteous anger. Don't believe it! Would our loving Father really incite Ahmad to leave you and Alesha because you failed to meet His perfect standards? That's as far from a true picture of God's character as the east is from the west.

If Satan (the real source of such thoughts) tries to make you anxious and fearful about God, remember that God does not keep a record of our sins.[9] If He did, no one, even the most religious, could survive His judgement. The truth is that Jesus the Righteous One died on the cross to meet God's demands for justice because of our sins. His death is 'payment in full' for all our wrongdoings, failures and acts of unfaithfulness.

God's 'paid in full' has cancelled out any record of debt for your sins, dear Kamila. In His sight you are debt-free, except for the debt of love.[10] So relax in God's presence, He holds nothing against you. Rejoice in hope of God's kindness and love for you everyday.

Third, it wouldn't also surprise me if *waves of rejection and betrayal* are breaking upon your heart. When these waves come crashing down upon our spirits, they leave us feeling weak, alone, friendless and hopeless.

What adds to the pain of rejection in a divorce is that it is more than just being left alone. Marriage engages two whole persons, each surrendering wholly to the other. When the marriage covenant is broken, we experience a betrayal of this total trust and commitment. This betrayal is without doubt one of the most distressing experiences anyone can have in this life.

So don't be shocked if you hear yourself shouting, 'It's just all so wrong! I've been his faithful wife. I've worked so hard to serve his every wish. And I gave him his beautiful daughter, Alesha. How could he betray my trust just because I changed my religious beliefs?'

Dear Kamila, I don't have any easy answers for you. It's inevitable that such cries and questions erupt from the depths of a troubled heart. But don't think of them as *sinful* eruptions, rather as the honest expressions of a wounded spirit. That's how God sees them.

God does not condemn you for being honest. Come to Jesus with your feelings of betrayal and rejection, asking Him to help bear their weight for the moment. You can do this because Jesus suffered the same trials. He was rejected by His own people, the Jews.[11] Judas Iscariot betrayed Him, his Rabbi and Master.[12] On the cross Jesus suffered wave upon wave of rejection and betrayal so that He could become for us a faithful High Priest to whom we could unburden our hearts at any time, about any issue.

So keep turning to Jesus at any time of day or night. Bring every emotion or thought that threatens to engulf you with its dark force. Stand up tall, not depending upon your own energy, but upon God's inexhaustible strength and power.[13]

Dear sister, while I don't know the details of God's plan for you and Alesha, I know that He has planned good things for you. He will give you a future together, rich with hope.[14] Don't let your heart be troubled. Trust and hope in God's faithfulness.[15]

We will keep asking our loving Father to provide your every need—physical, emotional and spiritual. And if we can help you in any practical way, please do not hesitate to contact us.

With our love for you, and a special affectionate hug for Alesha from both of us.

Your brother and friend,

Graham

Notes:

[1] John 14:16-18
[2] 2 Corinthians 1:3, 4
[3] Romans 5:3, 4; James 1:12; 1 Peter 1:6, 7
[4] Matthew 5:10-12
[5] Psalm 141:1, 2; Isaiah 38:5
[6] Philippians 4:19
[7] Psalm 145:14-19; 2 Corinthians 9:8; Hebrews 13:5, 6
[8] Psalm 68:19; 1 Peter 5:7
[9] Psalm 130
[10] Romans 13:8
[11] John 1: 11
[12] Luke 22: 4-6
[13] Habakkuk 3:19
[14] Jeremiah 29:11-13
[15] John 14:1

EIGHTEEN

A TREE BEARING GOOD FRUIT

Dear Joseph and Asminah,

As I begin this letter, I'm recalling our last visit to you. How special it was to see my former student now as a mature and caring husband and a father of three beautiful children. Times have changed, haven't they, my good friend? No more university assignments, but plenty of other assignments to take care of. Am I right?

Joseph, you are like a tree that is bearing *good* fruit.[1] I thank God for all He has been doing in your life since your university days. And dear Asminah, though I didn't know you as a student, I have seen in our visits to your home that you are a caring and responsible wife and mother.

Thank you Joseph, for your recent phone call. It's always good to hear your voice. Thanks for remembering us and for inquiring about our needs.

Since our chat together, God has placed a number of matters on my heart to share with you. I thought I'd write individual messages to each of you. Joseph, I hope you won't mind if I begin with Asminah.

Dear Asminah, whenever we visit, you make us feel that we are now *your* friends, not just Joseph's friends. Though we hold different beliefs, you always welcome us. Thank you most sincerely for opening your heart to us.

I also wanted to tell you how much we respect you for your conviction *not* to become a Christian just to make Joseph or your in-laws happy. We also respect you for your stance towards the ladies from Joseph's church when they tried to push you into becoming a follower of Jesus.

Asminah, we were upset when Joseph told us about their surprise visit and their half-teasing, half-serious comments asking when you would become a Christian. I can understand why their visit left you feeling so hurt and angry.

Please forgive them for their lack of sensitivity. I don't question the sincerity of their motives, but I certainly do not agree with their method of approach. Let me assure you, dear Asminah, that Jesus never tried to win followers by using psychological pressure or force. He called people to follow Him using clear words and a compassionate tone of voice.

And He always gave people the freedom to choose *not* to follow Him—which sometimes happened after He had done a miracle or taught about God's kingdom. Not everyone believed. Even if they walked away without believing, Jesus did not react angrily, nor did He compromise His message in order to win their acceptance.

So, dear Asminah, whenever we Christians offend you with our words or by our wrong attitudes, please keep in mind that the *real* Christian message is about Jesus, not about weak and failing Christians.

Now to you, Joseph. As I told you the other day on the phone, I am encouraged by your commitment to your family. Not every wife and child is blessed with a husband and father who takes his home responsibilities as seriously as you do. You'd agree with that, wouldn't you, Asminah?

However, I know from experience that fulfilling these roles isn't always smooth-sailing. I imagine that you have days when you are assailed with doubts, when all your diligence and hard work appears to be bearing little or no fruit.

For example, you may doubt your authority as a leader in your home when your children seem deaf to your good advice. But dear Joseph, God has promised that if we sow good seed, even with tears, we will reap a harvest of righteousness.[2]

Let me illustrate this by highlighting the challenge to instil thankfulness into our children's minds. This isn't just a good tradition but an attitude that Jesus Himself taught and lived.[3] But it doesn't come naturally because people are by nature self-centred. So you shouldn't be amazed when you need to remind your children to be thankful.

You can start by training them in everyday situations to be thankful to you, as their parents, and to each other, whenever something is done for them. As they learn to be thankful for small, everyday blessings, they will grow to be thankful to God for His special gifts, such as their health, their food, and above all for Jesus, God's most special gift of all.

Travel presents another opportunity to train your children how to be thankful for God's care and protection. I remember your telling us about your family visits to Asminah's mother. Maybe you already do this, but I suggest that you pray together with your family for God's protection when you are about to set off. After you have returned home safely, gather your family together and thank Him for watching over your trip.[4]

Dear Joseph, as you pray these spontaneous prayers of thanksgiving, you are depositing a rich knowledge of God and His ways in the minds of your children. You are passing on to them a heritage of great worth. You are also demonstrating a living faith in God—that being a follower of Jesus isn't about doing various 'religious duties' but about walking through each day in reliance upon a loving God who is actively and purposefully intervening in your daily circumstances *for your good.*[5]

While on the subject of prayer, allow me to highlight your responsibility as leader of your household to pray for yourself and your family. Yes, being a godly husband and father is often sheer hard work. Every day you face challenging situations for which you need divine discernment and wisdom.[6] You can respond simply by asking Him for wisdom and help. It's no more complicated than that!

You will also want to pray for your family's needs—Asminah's and your children's. Have you ever thought that by praying faithfully and regularly for your family you are working with God? That's true, Joseph, because prayer is the way God works to channel His countless spiritual and material blessings into your household.

The other equally important aspect of your spiritual leadership in the home is your personal responsibility to know God's Word, then to train your children to know God and to walk in His ways.[7]

You are like a 'builder', Joseph—a fellow-worker with God. And for your building materials God has given to you His Word of truth. By reading and meditating upon God's Word each day, and then by teaching and training your children to love and obey God's truth, you are building into their lives the principles for living that will keep them steadfast in the face of life's many storms.[8]

All of us, including our children, hear, read and see messages that are often in direct conflict with God's truth and God's ways. This is the world that we and our children engage every day. Take the materialistic influences that drive the advertising industry: We can't escape the constant message that we must buy this or that in order to be happy and successful in life.

You and I know that this message is a lie. In real life, no one is truly happy except those who know Jesus and obey His commands.[9]

With so many opposing messages, it's imperative that you let the light of God's truth illuminate your mind,[10] and then you can direct your family in God's ways. This is the only way that you will all enjoy true happiness, individually and as a family.

So, dear Joseph, take time each day amid all your busyness to open your Bible. Its truths will increasingly shape your thoughts and equip you to speak and act wisely as the father and leader of your household.

Your study of God's Word will then lead you to know and communicate the Bible's central message—concerning Jesus. Above all other ways, Jesus alone is the *Way* that leads us safely home to the Father. Above all other beliefs, Jesus alone is the *Truth* that sets us free from Satans's lies and bondages. Above all other philosophies of life, Jesus alone is the *Life* that fills our lives with true dignity, meaning and purpose.[11] There is no other truth more wonderful than this—God's Good News.

May God keep you faithful in carrying out the weighty responsibilities that He has committed to you. I also pray that He will bless you both, dear Asminah and Joseph, in your life together, in your relationship with each other. Though you may differ in your religious beliefs and practices, keep growing in love, trust and esteem for one another—just as you have been doing.

I look forward to our next visit. Hopefully we can organize this during next year's long vacation. Until then, please give each of your children a hug from Auntie Frieda and Uncle Graham.

Yours affectionately,

Graham

Notes:

[1] John 15:1-5; Galatians 5:22, 23

[2] Psalm 126:5, 6

[3] Matthew 14:19; 15:36; 26:26, 27; Luke 17:12-16; John 11: 41

[4] Psalms 121:7, 8; 91:9-11

[5] Romans 8:28

[6] James 1:5

[7] Deuteronomy 6:6, 7; 11:18-21; 29:29; 32:46; Psalm 78:1-8

[8] 1 Corinthians 3:11-15; 1 Peter 1:23-25

[9] Psalm 1; Matthew 5:1-12

[10] Psalm 119:130

[11] John 14:6; 3:16, 36; 8:36; 10:10; 11:25, 26

Answers for Your Marriage
by Bruce & Carol Britten

A book for those who are married or soon to be married dealing with issues such as love, romance, sex education, child raising, avoiding aids. This book answers all the above questions and many more. Really a practical guide for marriage and family life.

Pages: 204 *Paper back*

Building a Marriage God's Way
by Juliet Thomas

'Marriage between a man and a woman in the presence of God is a covenant with permanence as its aim.' To build a marriage God's way requires much more than finding the right mate. It requires also being the mate. To be forewarned is to be forearmed.

Pages: 116 *Paper back*